SPARK YOUR in CAREER

ADVERTISING

by Randi Zuckerberg

SPARK NOTES

Spark Publishing
A Division of Barnes & Noble
120 Fifth Avenue
New York, NY 10011
www.sparknotes.com

Library of Congress Cataloging-in-Publication Data

Zuckerberg, Randi.
   Spark your career in advertising / [by Randi Zuckerberg].
      p. cm.—(Spark your career)
   ISBN-13: 978-1-4114-9813-6
   ISBN-10: 1-4114-9813-5
   1. Advertising—Vocational guidance. I. Spark Publishing. II. Title.

HF5828.4.W65 2007
659.1023—dc22
                           2006100612
Please submit changes or report errors to www.sparknotes.com/errors.

Printed and bound in the United States.

10 9 8 7 6 5 4 3 2 1

CONTENTS

PART I: INDUSTRY SNAPSHOT

PART II: HOW TO BREAK IN

SPARK YOUR CAREER in CAREER

ADVERTISING

FOREWORD

by Rick Boyko

There is no single, straight, or true path into advertising. Some enter the business with a background in journalism, others with art or film work behind them. Some even come into it with law or medical degrees. In fact, I'm one of the few people I know who actually wanted to be in advertising from an early age. But that's what's so exciting about this business: You meet and work with so many interesting people from diverse backgrounds, all driven to create something that will connect with the brand and its consumer. Most people think that advertising is only about selling and marketing, but it is much more. It is about ideas, strategy, media, design, filmmaking, storytelling, and, in the end, creating culture.

Think of such icons as the Jolly Green Giant, Ronald McDonald, the Geico Gecko, and the Pillsbury Doughboy, just to name a few. All were created not by the brands they represent, but by the advertising agencies working with those brands. Apple's "Think Different," Nike's "Just Do It," Dove's "Real Beauty"—all are embedded in the popular culture, and, again, all the work of inventive advertisers.

Few careers will afford you the opportunity to communicate with and impact as large of an audience as the advertising industry, and there hasn't been a more exciting time to enter the business since the 1960s. Why? Because not since the golden age of television has there been a legitimate new medium that can reach people everywhere. Now we have countless new ways to engage and intersect with an audience: DVRs, MP3s, podcasting, and blogging, not to mention Web 2.0 and cell phone displays—the so-called "third screen." What's more, the consumer controls these mediums, deciding what and when they watch and how they interact with what they see. In turn, advertisers are creating ads that are more engaging, entertaining, unique, and innovative than ever before.

I spent 32 years in the advertising business before leaving it in 2003 to head up the number one–ranked graduate program in advertising at Virginia Commonwealth University. I didn't leave the industry because I was tired of it, but because I had always said advertising is a young people's business. As an educator, I view the future of this business through a student's eyes every day. As technology advances by leaps and bounds, that future is wide open. Advertising has always thrived on breaking molds and crossing boundaries, and the industry is shaped by creative, innovative individuals willing to wrestle with the possibilities. There's no better time to be part of it all than right now.

Rick Boyko
Director, VCU Adcenter
Former Chief Creative Officer and Co-President,
Ogilvy & Mather Worldwide, Inc.
Richmond, Virginia
2007

INTRODUCTION

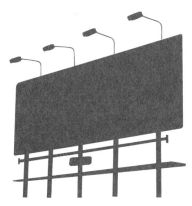

The cool, laid-back offices, the star-studded gala events, the outrageous parties, the tons of money being tossed about. What's *not* to like about advertising? Plus it's fantastically innovative to boot. In this age of computer wizardry, the Jolly Green Giant is no longer the benchmark of sophisticated image promotion.

The world of advertising is way bigger than the slick corporate executives, hipster art folks, and well-known celebrity spokespeople. For every Nike ad featuring LeBron James, there are hundreds of brochures and direct-mail pieces that are also part of the campaign. From billboards to bumper stickers, from the Ford Focus to Fran's Fabric Farm, advertising comes in all shapes and sizes. And behind the scenes there are people making the deals happen, researching the market, writing the ads, and testing the target audience.

But while advertisements may be for everyone, advertising isn't. Breaking into the industry is hard. If you've picked up this book, we know you dream of touching the masses. The question is: How are you going to make yourself stand out from the thousands of other eager souls so that *your* dream is the one that actually becomes a reality? The answer: hard work, and reading this book.

Spark Your Career in Advertising will tell you what you need to know to make it big on Madison Avenue. You'll get a crash course on the industry landscape, complete with a description of all the major players. We'll give you the skinny on the best sources to get up-to-date information on industry happenings. Never written a résumé or cover letter before? We've got you covered there too. We'll show you the way to a killer internship or the job of your dreams and how you can create a powerful network of contacts—even if your only prior advertising experience was Xeroxing flyers to promote your band's last show.

And if you land a job—scratch that. *When* you land a job, we'll tell you what working in advertising is really all about. Long hours, low pay, and some serious grunt work go hand in hand with the hip décor, outrageous perks, and rockin' parties. For those who are willing to put in the effort and the energy, an incredibly dynamic and exciting career awaits you. And we're going to get you there.

TOP 10 SIGNS YOU WERE BORN TO WORK IN ADVERTISING

1
As a child, you played "ad agency" with your favorite stuffed toys, the Energizer Bunny, Chester Cheetah, and the Michelin Man.

2
While your friends were checking out the latest prom wear in *Seventeen*, you were reading Rance Crain's columns in *Advertising Age*.

3
You've dressed as David Ogilvy for the past 15 Halloweens.

4
Your opinions on movies and TV shows always include a critique of product placement.

5
Instead of White Stripes and U2 posters, the walls of your room are plastered with "Got Milk?" ads.

6
You feel cheated by one-hour TV specials that have no commercial breaks.

7
For the past 10 years, you've been petitioning your local cable company to televise the One Show Awards.

8
You can't wait to apply as a contestant for the first season of *America's Next Top Account Executive*.

9
You were terribly disappointed when Orlando Jones jumped from 7-Up commercials to a legitimate movie career.

10
When your sister got engaged, you ran a viral marketing campaign complete with poster ads, streaming videos on MySpace and YouTube, and a GwenGetsHitched.com promo site.

PART I: INDUSTRY SNAPSHOT

1

HOW IS THE INDUSTRY DIVIDED?

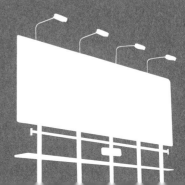

Most people dream of seeing their name in lights. Advertisers dream of seeing their *ideas* in lights. If you want to get into advertising, you long to see your work displayed on the largest neon billboard in Times Square or broadcast during the hottest event in the Olympic Games. You schedule your Super Bowl bathroom breaks to coincide with the game so you won't miss the commercials. You've been collecting Absolut ads and Think Different posters since you were in grade school. You even know where you'll line up your Effie, One Show Pencil, and Cannes Lion. The only question that remains: How do you get in?

THE BREAKDOWN

Agencies can be divided into three subcategories: full-service advertising, boutiques, and specialized agencies.

- **Full-service agencies** are large corporations that clients hire to research, plan, and create ad campaigns from start to finish.

- **Boutique agencies** are smaller companies that tend to focus solely on the creative elements of an ad campaign, producing trendier, riskier ads than full-service agencies. Boutique agencies tend not to perform other advertising services such as market research and distribution.

- **Specialized agencies** cater to niche sectors of the economy, such as healthcare or finance, or to specific groups of consumers that have their own buying trends, such as African Americans or pre-teens.

Each sector of the advertising industry has its own challenges and rewards, so it's important to determine which type of agency would best suit you.

FULL-SERVICE AGENCIES

Companies, such as Ford or Nike, want someone to manage every aspect of their ad campaign creation process so they hire a **full-service agency.** The largest full-service agencies may have more than 50 clients with teams of 10 to 25 employees assigned to each one. Full-service agencies also have incredible media resources: broadcast production departments, print production labs, and access to the best software and design tools. While they are more fun and laid-back than a typical Fortune 500 company, full-service ad agencies tend to have a very corporate atmosphere compared to smaller agencies.

Notable Ads

For most of the second half of the twentieth century, full-service agencies have dominated advertising. Full-service ad agencies have created most of the classic ads you've seen and remembered, from the DeBeers' "A Diamond is Forever" campaign to the Energizer Bunny. Many of these campaigns catapulted a brand to number one or helped launch an entirely new industry. Here are some of the most enduring ads created by full-service agencies:

> Campbell's Soup's "Mmmm mm good" (BBDO, 1930s)
> Marlboro's the Marlboro Man (Leo Burnett, 1955)
> Maxwell House's "Good to the Last Drop" (Ogilvy, Benson & Mather, 1959)
> Volkswagen's "Think Small" (DDB, 1959)
> Wisk Detergent's "Ring Around the Collar" (BBDO, 1968)
> Burger King's "Have it Your Way" (BBDO, 1973)
> Miller Lite's "Tastes Great, Less Filling" (McCann-Erickson Worldwide, 1974)
> Absolut Vodka's The Absolut Bottle (TBWA, 1981)
> Apple Computer's "1984" (Chiat/Day, 1984)
> Nike's "Just do it" (Wieden+Kennedy, 1988)
> Mastercard's "Priceless" (McCann Erickson Worldwide, 1998)
> Anheuser-Busch Budweiser's "True" (DDB Worldwide, 2000)
> Panasonic's "Ideas for Life" (Grey Worldwide, 2002)
> McDonald's "I'm Lovin' It" (Leo Burnett, 2003)
> American Express' "My Life" (Ogilvy & Mather, 2006)

Personality Profile

Most full-service agencies are large and hierarchical and require a requisite amount of trudging through the ranks on your way to success. Take a look at the following list—if the descriptions sound like you, you may fit in well at a full-service agency.

- **You never skip the commercials.** You find ads fascinating. They excite you. You look forward to living, breathing, and dreaming them. For the chance to be part of the process, you would be willing to spend months creating direct-mail postcards for a retail store or researching buffalo burgers.

- **"Ambition" is your first, middle, and last name.** Full-service agencies can be cutthroat. They are filled with young go-getters willing to go 10 extra miles and eager to receive recognition and earn promotions. You'll do whatever it takes to make it to the top, even if it means slogging through the more mind-numbing duties for the first few years.

- **You're not in it for the money.** You're prepared to spend the first few years of your professional life making little money, possibly in a large city where the rent and cost of living is up to your eyeballs. You don't mind playing pauper for a few years, secure in the knowledge that if you're really good at what you do, you will eventually be living like a prince.

- **You're flexible.** Getting noticed in a large company requires flexibility and the willingness to work long hours. You know that you will sometimes have to work late, and you're willing to free up your evening at a moment's notice. You won't get stressed out when you have to cancel on a friend or stop taking that evening ballet class that meets three times a week.

- **And gosh darn it, people like you!** You are a people person and a mastermind at negotiating different and sometimes difficult situations. Half your job will be persuading and cajoling clients, and higher-ups will want evidence that you're a first-rate persuader and cajoler.

Job Culture

Step into an ad agency and you'll feel the buzz and energy in the air—creative minds hard at work, art directors hurrying off to photo shoots in exotic locales, and executives gearing up for black-tie awards functions. But advertising isn't all fun and games. Compared with their smaller, more narrowly focused counterparts, full-service agencies move at a swift pace where navigating people and personalities is pivotal and the bottom line is law.

- **Twelve-hour days are the norm.** Appearances can be deceiving. Although the giant Kool-Aid Man in the lobby or the pinball machines on the second floor may give the impression of a fun and whimsical atmosphere, agency life can be intense, with long hours and low salaries. It's not unusual to get to your desk by 9:30 or 10 A.M. and find yourself in the exact same place 12 hours later. And that one-hour lunch break? More often than not, you'll eat lunch at your desk while simultaneously juggling 20 different tasks: writing the agenda for your weekly team meeting, finishing a PowerPoint presentation, returning urgent phone calls, and so on.

- **Guess who gets to do the filing?** Yes, we know that you graduated at the top of your class. But no matter who you are or where you've been, you'll get the ugly jobs when you're a newbie. Prepare for photocopying, scheduling, note taking, updating portfolios, and managing small projects. But trust us that hands-on is the best way to learn in the advertising world. Larger companies can mean greater exposure, and as you work your way up—and with hard work and a little luck, you'll move up quickly—you'll establish relationships with clients, participate in the creative process, help out with photo and commercial shoots, attend media parties, and manage larger projects.

- **Whenever you get comfortable, you'll need to think about moving.** Large full-service ad agencies offer employees a great deal of mobility within the company, between departments, clients, and even corporate locations. This provides employees with a tremendous opportunity to work on different projects and become experts in multiple areas.

- **Today's bottom-feeders will be tomorrow's creative directors.**
  Never underestimate the importance of the friendships you forge
  with your fellow entry-level employees. You may be impoverished
  coworkers on the bottom rungs of the company ladder right now,
  but you'll be the movers and shakers of the industry before you
  know it!

From entry-level to CEO

Shelley Lazarus, CEO of Ogilvy & Mather Worldwide, began thinking about
a career in advertising during her senior year at Smith College. In 1970,
she got an MBA from Columbia, where she was one of four women in her
graduating class. Within a year she joined Ogilvy in a junior role and
rose up through the ranks, earning accolades for her work with Avon,
Campbell's Soup, and Ralston Purina Co. She landed the multimillion-
dollar IBM account, securing exclusive control of all their advertising for
Ogilvy & Mather. When American Express, O&M's largest client, threatened
to leave, it was Lazarus who brought them back. She became CEO in 1997
and is now widely considered the most powerful woman in the business.
Says Radhika Dewan, account planner at O&M, "One of the things that
attracted me most to Ogilvy was the leadership of Shelley Lazarus and
Carla Hendra [co-CEO of Ogilvy North America]. It is so inspiring to see
women who worked their way up from junior positions to advertising
icons, and yet still manage to balance both career and family life."

The Major Players

A 2006 report by *AdAge* identified the following full-service agencies as
the top 10 most profitable in advertising.

- **J. Walter Thompson (JWT),** jwt.com
  Currently headquartered in New York City, J. Walter Thompson
  brought in $470 million in revenue in 2005, making it the most
  profitable American advertising agency. Major clients include HSBC,
  Ford, Shell, Pfizer, Unilever, and Vodafone. JWT prides itself on being
  socially conscious and a great place to work for all employees. JWT is
  part of the WPP family of ad agencies.

- **McCann Erickson Worldwide Advertising,** mccann.com
  With revenue topping $435 million in 2005, McCann maintained
  its position as one of the top three ad agencies in the country.
  Headquartered in New York City, the company's clients include
  Xbox, Intel, and Maybelline. The famous MasterCard "Priceless"
  campaign is one of its more enduring campaigns.

- **Leo Burnett Worldwide,** www.leoburnett.com
  A longtime industry giant headquartered in downtown Chicago, in
  2005 Leo Burnett brought in more than $350 million in revenue.
  Leo Burnett has worked with clients such as Wrigley's and Kellogg's
  and has produced such memorable campaigns as "I'm Lovin' It" for
  McDonald's and "Nice Altoids." Leo Burnett has also created such
  well-known icons as the Jolly Green Giant, the Marlboro Man, Tony
  the Tiger, and the Pillsbury Doughboy.

- **BBDO Worldwide,** bbdo.com
  BBDO is a prized gem in parent company Omnicom's crown. This
  New York City agency increased its 2004 profits by a significant 12
  percent to $280 million in 2005. Major clients it has worked with
  include Pepsi, Volkswagen, Aquafina, Wrigley's, and Guinness. It also
  came up with the award-winning "Volcano" ad for DaimlerChrysler's
  Jeep in 2006.

- **Ogilvy & Mather Worldwide,** www.ogilvy.com
  Led by the most powerful woman in advertising, this agency, which
  is headquartered in New York City, has worked with clients such as
  American Express, IBM, Dove, Motorola, Nestlé, and many other
  blue-chip household brands. One of its most popular campaigns is
  American Express's "Don't Leave Home Without It" series.

- **DDB Worldwide,** ddb.com
  DDB, a New York City agency, increased its revenue by more than
  13 percent in 2006 to over $260 million. Yet it has retained its
  small-agency feeling, with an atmosphere that employees describe as
  comfortable, friendly, and family oriented. Major clients have included
  Budweiser, McDonald's, Volkswagen, Dell, and ExxonMobil.

- **Grey Global Group,** grey.com
  This WPP family agency came into existence in 1917 when founder Larry Valenstein took a $100 loan from his mother and started a direct-mail company. The company now has over 10,000 employees, making it one of the largest full-service agencies. Headquartered in New York City with locations around the world, it brought in $250 million in 2005. Its clients run the gamut from the Olive Garden and Diageo Liquors to Nokia, Warner Bros., and Proctor & Gamble.

- **Draftfcb,** fcb.com
  This powerhouse Interpublic agency has gone through a lot of changes in 2006, merging with sister company Draft (a specialist in direct and digital marketing) to form the Draftfcb Group, headquartered in New York City. Clients include Coors, Kraft Foods, Quaker Oats, and Merrill Lynch.

- **Publicis,** www.publicis-usa.com
  Publicis, which began in London in 1906, has made an art of revitalizing old brands. It revived Proctor & Gamble's bath tissue brand Charmin, made Lancôme relevant to a younger audience, brought back the popularity of the PowerBar, and helped T-Mobile emerge as a latecomer in a highly competitive market. With offices still located on London's famous Baker Street, Publicis also has branches worldwide, including six in the United States.

- **Saatchi & Saatchi,** www.saatchi.com
  In 2005, Saatchi & Saatchi increased its revenue by 8 percent to move past fellow full-service agency Young & Rubicam (Y&R) to take the #10 spot. It is headquartered in New York City and has worked with brands such as Visa, Sony, Lexus, HP, and Toyota. Its London office, the home of the original agency, has its own onsite pub named after the firm's most famous ad, "The Pregnant Man," created for the U.K.'s Health Education Council to encourage the use of contraceptives.

HOLDING COMPANIES

In recent years, many large full-service ad agencies have consolidated under even larger, publicly traded umbrella corporations. The largest of these monster holding companies include the following:

- WPP (Ogilvy & Mather, Grey Worldwide, JWT, Y&R), wpp.com
- Omnicom Group (BBDO, DDB Worldwide), omnicomgroup.com
- Interpublic Group (FCB, McCann-Erikson), interpublic.com
- Publicis Groupe (Leo Burnett, Saatchi & Saatchi, Publicis), publicisgroupe.com

Holding companies work to keep their individual ad agencies separate enough that each agency maintains its individual culture and competing clients don't feel threatened. Employees of holding companies tend to have limited contact with people in their sister agencies, and agencies within the same holding company may find themselves contending for clients or working on competing brands.

BOUTIQUE AGENCIES

Boutique agencies are smaller companies that usually focus solely on creating ads, without the research, media planning, or market analysis services that full-service agencies provide. Often founded by former creative directors from full-service agencies, boutiques make their own rules, have less rigid hierarchies, and tend to attract more artsy, highly creative individuals to their ranks.

Even in the '50s and '60s, the early days of full-service agencies, solo creatives were breaking off and starting their own shops, such as Doyle Dane Bernbach and Wells Rich Greene. This trend picked up speed in the '80s, when a number of smaller boutiques emerged to defy the monster holding companies that were merging many larger agencies at the time. Many of these boutiques eventually went out of business because of economic downturns and the dotcom bust of the late '90s. Some survived, however, and others have found new footholds in the emerging online and international markets, carrying on their founders' legacy of renegade

Doyle Dane Bernbach began as a boutique "start-up" in 1949, then merged with Needham Worldwide in 1986, eventually becoming the advertising giant DDB Worldwide.

creative freedom. But advertising is a cyclical industry, and now holding companies are buying up all or parts of these smaller agencies, though even these agencies still function rather independently.

Got boutique?

The award-winning California Milk Board "Got Milk?" campaign is a boutique conception started in 1993 by Goodby, Silverstein & Partners. The original "Aaron Burr" spot, in which a history fanatic can't answer a radio trivia contest because his mouth is stuck with peanut butter, was exceedingly popular and was named one of the 10 best commercials of all time in a 2002 *USA Today* poll. Goodby, Silverstein & Partners agency is now credited with reviving a slumping milk industry and has grown greatly as a result. According to the official "Got Milk?" website, the campaign has over 90 percent recollection among Americans and has even become a multimillion-dollar licensing property, spawning apparel, paraphernalia, and parodies. In 2006, the tagline "Toma Leche" made its debut, bringing the campaign to a whole new Spanish-speaking market.

When you step inside a boutique agency, with the fiberglass walkways suspended high in the air, the bright orange walls, or the leopard-print sofas, you know that you're in a place where creativity thrives. When clients want a complete brand overhaul or an infusion of edgier, more inspired ideas, they turn to the boutiques, which are known for creating innovative, avant-garde campaigns. Some clients simultaneously employ full-service agencies and boutiques to maximize the breadth and number of creative possibilities. However, as technology continues to alter the advertising landscape, a growing number of clients are looking solely to these fresher, more flexible boutiques over larger, more established agencies.

Notable Ads

Clients hire boutiques because they want to take chances, and boutiques respond with campaigns that can capture a hip, up-to-the-minute feeling and are more attention grabbing than those created by their large agency counterparts.

Some recent ads from boutique agencies include the following:

- Reebok, "Beats and Rhythms of Sports" (The Arnell Group, 2006)
- Converse, "Game Face" (Butler, Shine, Stern & Partners, 2006)
- Burger King, "The Giant King" (Krispin Porter & Bogusky, 2005)
- Old Navy, group dancing ads (StrawberryFrog, 2004)
- Johnnie Walker, "Keep Walking" (Bartle Bogle & Hegarty, 2003)

From full-service to boutique

Before 2005, Motorola was a high-profile client of Ogilvy & Mather. But the company made waves that year by also hiring independent boutique agencies, such as 180 in Amsterdam, to handle some of its product-specific campaigns. In a similar move the prior year, MasterFoods USA dropped Grey Worldwide and handed a major campaign for Dove to creative boutique Nitro. Nitro played off of Dove's reputation as a silkier, smoother chocolate to position the candy as an everyday indulgence, not just a mere snack food. Nitro's original and much-discussed commercial features a woman arriving home from work in business dress, toting a Dove product in a shopping bag. Passing through a lush, silky curtain, she emerges barefoot in a flowing brown robe and reclines on a sofa, where she blissfully eats her chocolates.

Personality Profile

Because boutiques have fewer employees than large agencies, it's hard to blend into the background. Of course, as a hot-shot ad prospect, you're probably hungry for the attention. Check out the following list of qualities to see if you have what it takes to make a splash at a boutique.

- **You think outside the box.** You're artsy and creative, with a unique style and perspective. This doesn't necessarily mean that your hair is dyed blue and you have 18 tattoos. Your creativity comes out in your quirky take on life and unusual approach to challenges.

- **If your house was on fire, you would grab your portfolio first.** Your **portfolio** truly defines you and your career. In the world of boutiques, art and risk go hand in hand, and your portfolio will be your ticket to fame, fortune, and maybe even your own company.

A **portfolio** is a collection of personal and professional work samples every hopeful creative uses to promote his or her unique style and ability.

- **You can't stand the corporate machine.** Full-service ad agencies are exciting places to work, but they are large, which means cubicles, organizational structure, and a more corporate atmosphere. Boutiques are the place to be if you're passionate about the advertising industry but feel most comfortable in a smaller, less traditional work environment.

- **You can't imagine doing anything else.** Sure, nobody loves making thousands of photocopies or getting yelled at by an unhappy client. But those annoyances pale in comparison to your shining moments of creativity and brilliance. You (and everyone who succeeds in the industry) really love what you do.

Job Culture

From the hip décor to the funky vibe, boutiques are designed to foster creativity. The fun, laid-back environment provides more inspiration than a drab collection of cubicles on the 38th floor of a stoic office building. At a boutique, you might have a converted kitchen appliance for a desk or a mobile work space in an open setting where you can move about freely.

- **Professional décor? What's that?** You can feel the fruits of imagination all around you. Mad Dogs & Englishmen, a creative boutique agency that closed in 2005, described its atmosphere as "corporate punk," complete with pool tables and big comfy sofas. Other agencies have aquariums or an iMac-only policy. And if a dress code exists at all, it'll likely be little more than a ban on nudity.

- **You'll deal with less pesky office politics.** Without middle managers, chief executives, or vice presidents of vice presidenting, boutiques don't spend much time and energy on office politics—a luxury you're not going to find at a full-service agency. No matter where you work, some degree of interpersonal choreography is required, but you're likely to find a more comfy, inclusive atmosphere at one of these agencies. If you're the kind of person who likes to work autonomously, without constant oversight and red tape, you'll love the straightforward nature of boutiques.

- **Get ready for long hours and low salaries.** Sound familiar? As is typical of the entire industry, hours at boutiques are long and entry-level salaries are low. And with a relatively smaller staff, you may be asked to shoulder a heftier load than at a full-service agency. You'll most likely work between 10 and 12 hours a day and some weekends.

- **Your title may be "coordinating-administrative-production assistant."** Entry-level employees at boutiques have responsibilities and opportunities their counterparts at full-service agencies never have. Over the course of the day, you may do everything from answering telephones to running important meetings with clients to designing ad campaigns as an art director.

- **NYC or Silicon Valley?** Boutique agencies share many of the fun and exciting aspects of a small startup—fewer employees in a smaller office space, more responsibility for all, and tremendous opportunities for innovation. But like their California Internet brethren, boutiques also share some of the stressful aspects, such as more risk. It can be hard to win clients and revenue when you're competing with the sheer manpower and resources available to big companies with lots of dough.

The Major Players

Global holding conglomerates would like nothing more than to snatch up these hot shops, and some have succeeded in adding one or more boutiques to their arsenal. However, most boutiques have remained independent. Here are some of the better-known agencies.

- **Bartle Bogle Hegarty,** bartleboglehegarty.com
  Founded in the early '80s in the United Kingdom, BBH has six offices worldwide, in New York, London, Singapore, Tokyo, Shanghai, and São Paulo. Together, these offices employ about 600 people. Despite BBH's relatively small size, the agency has attracted major global brands, including Audi, Johnny Walker, Levi Strauss, British Airways, Baileys, Smirnoff, and AXE. BBH has been named Agency of the Year twice at Cannes.

- **StrawberryFrog,** www.strawberryfrog.com
StrawberryFrog is an independently owned advertising agency founded by three partners. With offices in New York, Tokyo, and Amsterdam, the agency competes with the larger, established firms by sparking cultural and popular movements for its brands with a unique approach it calls "Total Engagement" (a combination of sophisticated marketing and grassroots PR). The agency has worked with clients such as Credit Suisse, Heineken, IKEA, Kohl's, Microsoft, Mitsubishi, Old Navy, MTV, Hoegaarden, and Sprint. Company employees call each other "frogs."

- **Mother,** www.motherlondon.com
With offices in London and New York and a staff of roughly 100 employees, the U.K.-founded boutique Mother takes a unique approach to advertising and to agency life in general. The Dr. Pepper ads that ask, "What's the worst that can happen?" where an innocent prom date may end in a wrestling match with the girl's father, have been running in the United Kingdom since they began in 2005 and are a good example of Mother's honest and somewhat snarky sensibilities. Rather than employing account management folks, the creative staff speak directly with the clients, and all work is conducted in an open-plan office (the London location is a converted fire station!).

In a *New York Sun* article, Paul LaVoie, founder and chief creative officer of Taxi, expresses his belief that 150 is the magic number of employees: "When a certain African tribe reaches 150 people, it sends two of its leaders out to start another tribe."

- **Taxi,** taxi.ca
Launched in 1992, this Toronto-based creative shop is dedicated to challenging convention in all media venues. Its self-described "media neutral" approach is embodied in campaigns that integrate print, online, broadcast, and outdoor advertising. The majority of Taxi's employees are in their 20s and early 30s. With offices in Toronto, New York, and Calgary, Taxi has worked with clients such as Microsoft, NASCAR, and Sunglass Hut. Within a year of opening the NYC offices in 2004, they cracked *AdAge*'s "10 Agencies to Watch" list and actually had to start turning down business.

- **Cliff Freeman & Partners,** clifffreeman.com
New York agency Cliff Freeman & Partners' simple goal is to combine an understanding of product truths with human needs to create campaigns that communicate brand individuality. This agency is the

brains behind the Little Caesar "Pizza, Pizza" campaign, and it has also done work for FoxSports.com, Snapple, Sports Authority, and Canada Dry. Canadian firm MDC Partners owns a 20 percent stake in the company, so it's not entirely independent.

- **Butler, Shine, Stern & Partners,** bssp.com
  A boutique agency located in Sausalito, California, BSSP is known for its creativity and innovation. Working with Converse in 2004, the agency pioneered the idea of asking customers to make and share videos about the product. To win BMW's business, Butler Partners filmed a video of staffers driving down historic Route 66 in a MINI.

Butler Partners recently created encrypted MINI ads designed exclusively for current owners of the car. Owners search in ads for web links to prizes and special events, enticing non-owners to get in the loop.

SPECIALIZED AD AGENCIES

Specialized agencies research and produce ad campaigns that target specific consumers or run in unusually complex markets. There are three main types of specialized agencies.

- **Industry-specific agencies** know the complicated ins and outs of government-regulated markets such as healthcare and nonprofits. Some agencies focus solely on political campaigns, while others focus on specialized industries, such as pharmaceuticals or industrial goods.

- **Demographic-specific agencies** focus on particular consumers, such as teenagers or Asian Americans. These agencies create ads for brands that would like to expand their presence in hard-to-reach yet large and powerful demographics.

- **Media agencies** place ads that other agencies have produced in the locations where they are most likely to reach a target audience. As media becomes more fragmented through advances in technology and consumers are given more choices about what to read and watch and how to spend their free time, specialized media agencies are ever more crucial to the success of an ad campaign. A few years ago, hardly

Where full-service agencies have an obligation to clients not to take on competing accounts, specialized agencies will often handle accounts for competing companies at the same time.

anyone knew about podcasting, TiVo, YouTube, blogs, or MySpace, let alone thought of using them as advertising platforms. Now, choosing a specialized media company that is familiar with these advancements and how to use them is almost as important as creating a great ad.

User-generated content and the new era of advertising

Advertising used to be about storytelling in a controlled, defined environment, like the 30-second commercial spot or a full-page magazine ad. Now brands are starting to let consumers tell the story themselves through company-sponsored groups and discussion forums on social networks, contests on video sites, and more. The money companies are spending in advertising on user-generated content sites, such as YouTube, Wikipedia, and Digg, is quickly increasing, even as companies scramble to discover the right way to use them. The advantage is in the ease of "sharing," as users discover exciting content that others have created and pass it along to their friends, who in turn pass it to their friends, and so on.

Some brands are scared to go there just yet, due to their fear of negative feedback or haphazard online placement that may give consumers the wrong message (having a life insurance ad placed on the Maxim website, for example). But other brands have jumped headfirst into this exciting and somewhat unpredictable space. Apple was the first to advertise on Facebook, a popular social networking site, where they created a sponsored group with a discussion board, information about their products, and weekly giveaways of iPods and iTunes songs. Although anticipating only modest results, their group generated a lot of buzz and ended up with over 600,000 members.

Notable Ads

Specialized agencies are . . . well . . . specialized, which means that the ads they produce generally appear in a . . . well . . . specialized market, as opposed to mainstream media. If you read healthcare magazines or watch narrowly focused television channels such as BET or the Food Network, you've most likely seen the work of one of these agencies. As an example, here are some notable ads created for the Latino market that were recently honored during the 2006 Hispanic Creative Advertising Awards.

- **California Milk Processor Board, "Teeth Town" (Grupo Gallegos):** Part of Grupo Gallegos's initial "Toma Leche" campaign, which brings the "Got Milk?" message to a Latin American audience, this spot reveals a town whose inhabitants use their calcium-enriched teeth to perform all of life's activities, from carrying briefcases to driving cars to playing tug-of-war. A diversion from the board's previous, more wholesome attempts to reach Spanish-speaking consumers (*famila, amor, y leche*; "family, love, and milk"), this spot's quirky sense of humor, which replicates the sensibilities of the original English-language commercials, proved to be successful with viewers.

- **Toyota's 4Runner, "Singers" (Conill):** Conill disguises this spot as a typical car commercial: The rugged Toyota 4Runner winds through a jungle scene with evocative chanting music in the background. Once the car stops at a small tribal village, it's revealed that the chanting is coming from the indigenous passengers sitting in the back seat, who reluctantly crawled out to join their fellow villagers. The commercial was rated as Toyota's most memorable in studies and was even adapted for use with English-speaking audiences.

- **Heineken, "Domino Tournament" (Vidal Partnership):** A clever use of a wildly popular Latino pastime, this spot features an International Dominos Tournament, where the Puerto Rican, Dominican, and Mexican players argue over the rules until the bar owner announces that everyone will get a Heineken once the tournament starts. Understandably, everyone immediately quiets down and gets ready to play.

- **Comcast CableLatino, "Taxi" (Grupo Gallegos):** This commercial, another clever play on cultural norms, features a Mexican tourist hailing a cab. Rather than jumping in the yellow taxi that stops for him, the tourist jumps in a green VW beetle, the typical taxi in Mexico, which pulls up behind it. The tagline *si extrañas México, ahora lo vas a extrañas un poco menos* ("If you miss Mexico, now you'll miss it a little less") introduces Comcast's new Latino channel.

- **Continental Airlines, "Beto" (Bromley Communications):**
  Illustrating a universal theme, this spot opens with a family waiting
  expectantly at an airport, complete with welcome signs, for a loved
  one to arrive. When Beto comes through the gate with outstretched
  arms, the family doesn't recognize him. The message: *Es hora de
  volver a casa más seguido. Más vuelos sin escalas a más destinos en
  Latinoamérica* ("It's time to return home more often. More flights to
  Latin American destinations.")

Personality Profile

Advertising is advertising, no matter where it's practiced. But more than at
other agencies, working in specialty advertising requires a certain degree
of obsession. Here are some of the qualities you'll need to enjoy the specialized life.

- **You enjoy delving deep.** You're the type of person who likes to buckle
  down and learn all the ins and outs of one industry.

- **You've been the in-the-know kid on the block since you were
  two.** Specialized media agencies must stay up-to-date with the latest
  trends to provide clients with the best marketing strategies available.
  You keep up with the latest CNET news and have always owned the
  coolest new gadgets.

- **You've got the skills to pay the bills.** You know a great deal
  about the specific people you are working with. If you want to work
  for an agency that focuses on Latino markets, for example, your
  Spanish language skills need to be excellent. If you want to work in
  a more technical industry, you must speak fluent technobabble. If
  you want to work in healthcare advertising, you should understand
  government regulations. You may not have previous experience in
  your area of choice, but you should be familiar with the way that
  community thinks and feels.

- **You are passionate, hardworking, yada, yada, yada.** Yes, we know
  you've heard this one before. And no, we're not just looking to fill

space. If you don't love what you do and if you're not willing to work your tail off, you won't get far in advertising, no matter what kind of agency you're with. That's a message worth repeating.

Job Culture

In a specialized agency, everyone is focused on one particular market within the larger advertising industry. Your role will be similar to the one you would have at a full-service ad agency, but your focus will be narrower. If you're working at an interactive media agency, prepare to be fully immersed in interactive media. (Warning: This immersion comes with invitations to some really awesome parties and gift bags!) If you're working at an Asian-interest agency, you should be prepared to hear more Japanese, for example, than English. And if you're working at a healthcare agency, get ready to hear medical jargon around the clock.

- **Your life will be a bubble.** Everyone you work with will have something in common—a passion for a particular field or a great deal of experience in that specialized industry. If you're working in a specialized government agency, you might find that your fellow employees talk about politics all day long, even during their lunch breaks. If you're working for a youth-centric company, you may find that everyone you work with is under 30. This shared vision will help you focus, but make sure to come up for air every once in a while.

- **Your employer will be small but fierce.** Specialized advertising agencies tend to be much smaller than 1,000-plus-employee full-service shops. This means access to clients and senior executives and some rewarding work even at entry levels. It also means higher expectations and more visibility for both your successes and your failures.

- **The agencies come in many forms.** Want to work for an independent company? Want to work for a small agency owned by a larger holding company? Whatever you want, you can find it in one of the specialized agencies. Specialty shops come in many types and sizes, which means that the job culture varies greatly from place to place.

Traditional media vs. interactive advertising

The relatively new phrase "traditional media" refers to television and radio commercials and print ads in newspapers and magazines—what used to be just called "media." Although there is a lot of talk in the industry about online, interactive, and emerging media, the reality is that traditional media still attracts the majority of ad dollars. Online advertising is an exciting new frontier, but Super Bowl spots will always get clients to shell out the big bucks.

For now. But with recent breakthroughs in technology and revolutions in the ways people approach the online experience, the old rules of advertising are being broken and new business models are forming every day. User interactivity is allowing a new level of dialog between company and consumer, a concept known as **Web 2.0**, and advertisers are taking note.

Many specialized agencies that focus on interactive advertising sprang up before traditional advertising giants had fully embraced the Internet. According to *AdAge*'s annual revenue rankings for 2006, these are the top three interactive agencies:

1. Avenue A/Razorfish (avenuea-razorfish.com), Seattle, $190 million (a 37 percent revenue increase from 2005!)

2. Sapient (sapient.com), Cambridge, Massachusetts, $176 million

3. Digitas (digitas.com), Boston, $155 million

Other big names in interactive advertising include Organic, Tribal DDB, AKQA, Leapfrog Online, and Carat Fusion. While some of these agencies focus more on media strategy and planning than creative execution of the actual ads, others closely integrate the creative, media planning, and digital production aspects of their campaigns. As the Internet changes and evolves, these companies must stay current and understand how to get the most value in areas such as search engine optimization and social networking.

Traditional media isn't going away, but it's going to have to share more of the pie in the future. Interactive advertising will grow exponentially as people spend more time online and clients respond by transferring large chunks of their budgets over to online advertising. It is a fantastic place for recent grads to begin their careers, since it's a great professional asset to actually be a part of the young Web 2.0 demographic that consumes social media and spends the majority of their day online.

66 The future isn't about the web or TV, just like it wasn't about print or TV in the past. People are going to consume all of it. TV won't go away, although its relative importance [in terms of advertising dollars] will be diminished. But even though times change and technology changes, people stay the same. One hundred years ago and 100 years from now, people will always respond to a good story. With ambient media, homemade viral videos, and blogging, advertising is more challenging but also more liberating. An advertiser has the opportunity to create ideas and tell stories in such an interesting way. The areas for creativity have multiplied in the last 20 years."

—**Ty Montague,** Chief Creative Officer
JWT

The Major Players

Listing and describing all of the specialized agencies that exist would fill an entire book. Just to give you an idea of the variety out there, here's a look at the specialized agency list of WPP, one of the largest umbrella companies.

HEALTHCARE AGENCIES

- **CommonHealth,** www.commonhealth.com
  CommonHealth began more than 30 years ago as one small agency, Ferguson, and quickly expanded to cover a large array of healthcare promotional, advertising, and marketing services. Its current clients include Listerine, RxCentric, Zantac, and Levitra.

- **Grey Healthcare,** ghgroup.com
  With over 40 offices in 21 countries, Grey Healthcare provides a wide variety of services for healthcare-specific clients. Grey Healthcare is run by CEO Lynn O'Connor Vos, who was recently awarded the Healthcare Businesswomen's Association Woman of the Year award in 2005. Its client list includes Advair, Cialis, Crestor, and Viramune.

MULTICULTURAL AGENCIES

- **Bravo Group,** thinkbravo.com
  Founded in 1980, Bravo is now one of the leading U.S. Latino

advertising agencies, with such major clients as AT&T, Mazda, and Banco Popular.

- **Kang & Lee,** kanglee.com
  A marketing firm specializing in the Asian American market since it was founded in 1985, Kang & Lee handles accounts for AT&T, Sears, Chivas Regal Scotch, the *New York Times,* and the NBA. Kang & Lee does a lot of business around the Chinese Lunar New Year, but its work is essentially hidden from mainstream American society because it places its advertising primarily in Asian-language media.

MEDIA AGENCIES

- **MindShare,** www.mindshareworld.com
  Created in 1997, MindShare offers services in strategic media planning, buying, negotiation, and execution. It has grown to more than 5,000 employees and has offices in nearly 100 countries, most recently opening MindShare Cambodia in the summer of 2006. Clients include Cisco, Lufthansa, Nike, and Volvo.

- **Mediaedge:cia,** www.mecglobal.com
  Mediaedge, which calls itself the "first global communications planning and implementation agency," has over 4,000 employees in 80 countries. It provides services in consumer insight and **ROI** (return on investment), communications and media planning, media buying, sponsorship, consulting services, product placement, and entertainment marketing. Mediaedge spends over $100 million per year on research and development, and handles such major brands as Campbell's, Canon, DHL, Sony Ericsson, Visa, and Yahoo!

Still think like a kid?

There are even specialized agencies for people like you. The Alloy Media & Marketing group includes a specialized agency dedicated to developing and executing marketing programs to reach college students, teens, and tweens. 360 Youth works with more than 1,500 clients each year. By using innovative approaches such as outdoor and guerrilla marketing, as well as traditional advertising, it reaches the youth market in school, on campus, in school newspapers, on social networks, in movie programs, on textbook covers, and anywhere else you might imagine.

As you can see, there's no shortage of options when it comes to deciding which type of agency would fit you best. Hopefully, this variety is exciting to you, not overwhelming. Whether your dream is to work in a 25-person office, incorporate your love of the Japanese language into your day job, or work on multimillion-dollar campaigns for the biggest of the big, there is an ad agency out there perfectly suited to you and your interests.

2

WHAT KIND OF WORK COULD I DO?

FROM THE CLIENT'S BRIEF TO THE CONSUMER'S BRAIN IN 6 EASY STEPS

Putting together a successful ad campaign involves more than just a good idea. It takes months of strategic and creative planning and execution. A high-profile project typically involves a staff of five to 15 people, sometimes more, every one of whom plays a key role in the campaign's success. Here is a basic blueprint for creating an ad.

1

The Client Brief   Every project begins with the client's decision to launch an ad campaign. The client comes to the ad agency with a business problem—"We want to challenge the leading soft drinks in the youth market"—hoping that the solution lies in branding, marketing, and creating the perfect ad. They present the basic parameters of the campaign—the budgets and desired outcome—and the agency runs the project from there.

2

Organizing the All-Star Team   The account executive leads the project. She receives the client brief and takes responsibility for getting the project done according to the client's budget, goals, and expectations. With input from the account exec, the creative director decides which copywriters and graphic designers would make the best team for the project, considering who has worked with this client before or is particularly suited for this market. The account exec also plans the schedule of deliverables, such as drafts of copy for the client to approve, keeping in close contact with the client throughout the process.

3

Creative Development   The creative team of art directors and copywriters comes up with multiple concepts for each project and pitches them to the client ("What if we had Mischa Barton drinking your cola?"). This might include potential taglines to carry the campaign and rough sketches or storyboards, depending on the project. In some cases, several possible campaigns will be **tested** against each other, using focus groups or online surveys and **animatics** to identify the strongest concepts in terms of brand linkage, intent to purchase, and likability. Once the leading concept is chosen, the creative team develops and revises, working closely with account management, which is in turn working closely with the client, until the winning concept is ready for production. If a commercial needs to be filmed, the creative team oversees the process from start to finish.

4

Media Planning   As the creative concept is being perfected, the media services department is researching and crunching numbers to figure out when and where the ad should run. Based on the target audience and client budget, media planners inform the creative process, guiding the execution of the campaign to maximize the target audience's exposure to the ads. The soft drink ad, meant for 13- to 18-year-olds, would be most effective in teen magazines, on TV channels such as MTV and Comedy Central, and on popular social networking websites, with a coordinated launch planned to coincide with the start of the new school year.

5

Production   Production may take place simultaneously with some of the other steps, such as media planning, depending on the exact component being produced. Television commercials need a lot of production time, while online banners and pop-up ads need very little. Working with the account exec, creative team, and media services to ensure accuracy and perfect timing for a launch, production brings the campaign to life.

6

Media Outlets   Finally, the campaign launches to the consumer. All systems go as the finished components are sent to the television stations, magazines, and websites where they're scheduled to run. The viewer absorbs it all—and hopefully buys tons of the soda as a result. Time to celebrate!

As you can see, there's a lot involved in coming up with a winning idea and turning it into an ad you see in *Rolling Stone*. The account management team works hand in hand with the creative and media teams, and dozens of professionals, from art directors to writers, from media analysts to media buyers, collaborate to create successful ads. The best news? There's always room for new talent and fresh ideas.

JOB CATEGORIES

Now that you have an idea of how a campaign might run, it's time to look at potential career paths in the industry. Advertising has roles for every personality type and skill set. Not an artist or a writer? Maybe you're meant to be an account executive who runs the show, acts as a liaison between client and agency, and keeps everyone happy. Or perhaps you belong in media services, deciding where and when the campaigns should run. In the largest agencies, you may find yourself performing a very specialized role in the development process, but in smaller ones, you'll be asked to wear many different hats.

There are three major areas of the advertising industry:

- Account Management
- Creative
- Media Services

We'll talk about these departments in depth before providing brief descriptions of the other departments that you may want to check out: Production, Research/Strategic Planning, Traffic, and New Business.

Having trouble deciding? The good news is you don't have to make up your mind right away. Many agencies now offer rotation programs in which recent college grads spend three to four months with each department.

ACCOUNT MANAGEMENT

Account managers manage all communication between the agency and the client. They are the completely frazzled yet almost impossibly chic folks you see running through the halls at lightning speed. When the client has a specific request, the account management team relays that desire convincingly and accurately to the creative team. If the creative team vetoes the idea, the account management team goes back to the client to explain. This challenging job requires passion, energy, and terrific people skills.

Large ad agencies typically have multiple account management teams, each of which focuses on one client or a subcomponent of that client. A huge company like IBM might have one team handling online ads, another handling print, and yet another handling sponsorship of events like the Olympic Games or the US Open. Each team is its own entity, but all of the teams communicate to ensure a consistent brand message.

Ad agencies' account management departments are usually very hierarchical, with new hires coming in as assistant account executives or, if it's a small agency or the new hire has some prior experience, as account executives. If you work really hard—we're talking 12-hour days and then some—you can get promoted fairly quickly from assistant account executive to account executive to account supervisor, on your way up to account director!

Account executives
do not:

- Write and design ad campaigns

- Decide where the ads will run

- Take the client out for dinner every single night

Personality Profile

People who go into account management love the business side of the industry. They enjoy the fast-paced nature of agency life, the challenges of meeting client demands, and the dynamics of working with a team. You may be picturing a drill sergeant barking out orders or a glorified waiter running back and forth between the kitchen and a table of six anxious diners, but account management is even more intense than that. As an account executive, you will be both consultant and partner to the client. You have to understand their business goals and obstacles, provide expertise on consumer behavior and the market, and come up with the best advertising solution possible.

You might be cut out for account management if you have some or all of the following characteristics.

- **You're the go-to person.** You can handle the stress of difficult clients, demanding deadlines, and a stubborn creative team. You relish life as the central unit of the client's strategic development. You want the excitement, the heartbreak, and the occasional glamour of the job. You know that although the days are hectic, there's nothing quite like going into a meeting with a killer idea that might change the way the world sees the client's brand.

- **You're a people person.** You are a seemingly endless fountain of positive thinking, charisma, and charm. You enjoy working with all kinds of people, even those that don't enjoy working with you.

- **You're the perfect blend of sugar and spice.** You know when to give in and when to push back hard. You're one part skillful negotiator, one part tough cookie, and two parts charmer.

- **You'll take the compliments *and* the blame.** You are comfortable taking responsibility for anything that goes wrong, even if it isn't remotely your fault. Because you're the contact, the client will vent to you and blame you for everything. However, the reverse is also true: You get to take credit for everything that goes off smoothly.

- **You love to multitask.** You enjoy working on 10 simultaneous projects with 10 different people. Account managers don't have the luxury of focusing in depth on one thing day in and day out. Every day is action packed.

- **You don't buckle under pressure.** You can stay calm when the client wants the revised drafts of the new print ad done yesterday, your boss is standing over you demanding a status report on another project, the art director is calling you every 30 seconds, and you have a meeting with media planning in four minutes. Bring it on.

The Workplace

At agencies large and small, the account teams are the businesspeople, so their departments are laid out in a more corporate fashion. You can usually read the hierarchy of job titles in the office layout. Interns, assistant account executives, and sometimes even account executives will typically be in cubes or pods (if it's an open floor plan), with more senior employees in surrounding offices.

There will be a cubicle somewhere in the office with your name on it, but don't expect to spend more than a few uninterrupted moments there. With calls to answer, bosses to report to (more than one, if you're at the entry level), and, as you move up, creative teams to instruct and clients to meet, you'll be constantly on the move. All this makes for one busy, busy employee and many long, long days.

With all the meetings, calls, and conversations that take place during regular business hours, chances are you won't get around to writing, proofreading, and administrative tasks until 5 P.M. comes around and your clients go home. Your friends may write you off, but it can be very economical to work late hours! Not only will you not be spending money by going out, but most companies will pay for your dinner and taxi ride home if you stay past 8 o'clock.

Putting in "face time"

Most of the time, when you're in the office until 8 P.M., it's because you actually have work to do. However, you'll sometimes need to stay late simply to let people know you're there. It may sound masochistic, but hanging around just so that your boss and coworkers don't think of you as the person who scoots at 5 P.M. every day can be good business practice. Some people wear their long hours like a medal, but their late nights at the desk may not mean that they are working harder than their more organized coworkers who leave at seven. You don't have to go to extremes, but proving dedication through endurance is an important way to get noticed. Now you know the terrible secret.

Before running for the hills, you should know that account management is not all work. Many account management teams play as hard as they work. The fast pace attracts a younger, more energetic crowd than do other departments. Happy hours and team bonding events are wild and plentiful.

66 We literally used any occasion we could—birthday, project launch, someone leaving the team, someone joining the team, someone running the marathon, anything—to party, and we partied hard! We'd start at 6 P.M. at our favorite bar around the corner from the office and could be found still out dancing, doing Jager shots, or singing karaoke well past 2 A.M. It was always fun coming in the next morning . . ."

—Anonymous Assistant Account Executive

The Salaries

Lots of money goes into advertising. Unfortunately, you won't be seeing it. At least not for a while. Eventually you'll make a suitable income, but initially your salary will be low, which can be tough if your heart is set on living in Manhattan or another major (and majorly expensive) city. Expect slightly more money if you have previous work experience or are relocating from across the country, but in general, the trade-off for a job in a glamorous industry means a low salary in the beginning.

According to the Bureau of Labor Statistics, as of 2006, entry-level assistant account executives earn approximately $32,000 to $35,000 a year, with benefits at all but the smallest companies usually including health insurance and paid vacation. Assistant account executives specializing in interactive/online markets tend to make slightly more than their television/print ad counterparts. Large companies will often offer team bonuses that may or may not trickle down to you, depending on the head of your team.

Unfortunately, it is common in the advertising industry to get a promotion without getting a raise. You could work at a place for three years, get two promotions, and earn exactly the same salary you did when you first started. As a result, agencies tend to have a lot of turnover, as employees realize that the best way to get a raise is to take their promotion and use it as leverage to get a higher salary at a competing firm.

Prospects

The need for entry-level employees in account management is constantly growing as new companies, markets, and products emerge. The job market these days is hot and advancement prospects are excellent. Larger agencies add account management jobs at all levels whenever they win new multimillion dollar accounts. And companies often prefer to promote from within, so if you find yourself working at a company that consistently wins new business, think twice before going somewhere else.

The majority of young account executives tend to gravitate toward television and magazine advertising for the high-profile, exciting, and reliable work. This creates a huge vacuum in certain areas, such as **direct-mail, direct marketing,** and (for now) **interactive marketing,** and agencies are desperate to fill the void with talent. Sometimes positions will open up with companies that specialize in direct and online marketing, but more often they are available in focused departments within larger ad agencies. If you are determined to work in traditional media, there are many more opportunities among the less sexy products than among the coveted beer, soft drink, and fashion brands. If you long to work for Budweiser, Coke, or Gap, take a number. But if you are open to working with any client, you will find opportunities galore. Large, diverse companies, such as Proctor & Gamble, have an immense and ever-growing variety of products, which means lots of jobs!

Because advertising is seen as a glamorous industry and because most jobs in ad agencies are not formally listed, getting an assistant account executive position is competitive. A high rate of turnover means that there may be no open jobs one week and three open jobs the next. The key is perseverance, networking, and educating yourself about the industry.

According to the U.S. Department of Labor, jobs in the advertising industry are expected to increase faster than the average for all occupations through 2014. (See bls.gov for more information.)

Job Titles

Every advertising agency is organized differently, but these titles are fairly standard.

- **Account Director**
  The account director is a high-level senior executive who reports directly to the agency's upper management. She helps with strategic

planning and operations and works closely with the agency's other executives and the senior-level clients to identify and meet profit goals. The account director is responsible for the performance of her department as a whole. She directs the account managers/supervisors who oversee the day-to-day operations of projects for specific clients. Account directors have often been at the same agency for many years and have developed a thorough knowledge of their agency's vision and culture.

- **Account Manager/Supervisor**

  This middle-management position reports to an account director and acts as superintendent of the day-to-day functions of one or more account executives who are directly managing a client's campaign. It is the supervisor's responsibility to make sure that each project is of high quality and adheres to an overall vision and, most important, that business is conducted in a way that makes the client happy. A large agency may have several account supervisors, each working with a different client or on separate projects for a single client. (For example, with a major credit card client, one account supervisor may oversee new card projects while another oversees customer loyalty programs.)

- **Account Executive**

  An account exec is in frequent contact with his supervisor for any concerns that come up as he coordinates between the internal teams working on a campaign and the client. He helps oversee the work of the creative team and media planners, maintains the schedule, and keeps the project on budget, all with aid from an assistant account executive. The jump to manager/supervisor usually comes after about two to three years in this position.

- **Assistant Account Executive**

  The assistant reports to an account executive and is responsible for everything from basic clerical tasks such as photocopying and filing to analyzing the work of competing brands. She attends internal (and sometimes client) meetings, works with creative and media teams, and learns the ins and outs of client service. Assistant account executive is

Direct-mail and online marketing move at a rapid pace, which means more projects and a constant demand for new assistant account executives.

typically stop number one for new grads, with a tenure of one to two years before that first promotion to account executive.

The Ground Floor

Recent college grads will probably start as assistant account executives reporting directly to the account executive or account manager. But in reality, you're working for everyone higher than you on your team, meaning you'll effectively have anywhere from one to 10 bosses.

Assistant account executives spend the first few months shadowing bosses, attending meetings in which they have no idea what is going on, and trying to absorb as much as possible. Lots of phone answering, photocopying, and other forms of grunt work are the norm. Eventually, assistants can work up to some real client contact and may be handed responsibility for the smooth operation of a small component of an ad campaign, such as creating a new version of an already-existing print piece or direct-mail postcard. More seasoned assistants will often manage a summer intern or two.

Because an entry-level job in account management requires fewer technical skills than a job in creative services or production and because there are more entry-level roles in this area to go around, account management is very popular for recent grads. Many agencies now offer year-long training programs in which recent grads rotate through different teams and products, often starting out in or spending the majority of their year with account management teams (see Chapter 5 for more on agency training programs). As long as you are smart, dedicated, and compulsively organized, you will learn everything you need to know on the job.

66 I didn't participate in an official training program; however, my boss volunteers my team to attend relevant conferences and seminars. It's amazing how much you pick up just through working through the processes once you start! At the AAE level, client contact is normally limited, but I've been lucky enough to build up to daily contact with the client via phone, and I visit their office about once a week."

—**Brooke Firchow,** Assistant Account Executive
DDB

CREATIVE

Creativity is the heart and soul of an agency, the idea factory that keeps the business running. Referred to collectively as "the creatives," people in this department are responsible for taking a client's idea and turning it into an actual ad campaign. Let the account management team be responsible for keeping the client happy—the creative team is focused on envisioning groundbreaking ads.

The creative department consists primarily of copywriters, who write the words, and art directors, who arrange those words in an appealing way. Each creative brings specific technical and artistic skills to a team, and as a result, the department is much less hierarchical than account management. A creative director heads up the department, overseeing the team, managing the workload, and helping out with some of the most high-profile pieces of work. Additional freelancers, such as artists, photographers, directors, and actors, may also be hired to help produce an ad.

Personality Profile

Creatives are typically bursting with great ideas—which is good, because they will have to come up with hundreds, even thousands of them over the course of their careers. If you have some or all of the following qualities, you might make a good creative.

- **You can't turn your brain off.** Your brain bubbles with a seemingly endless fountain of fresh ideas. You draw inspiration from everything: travels, colors, cities, music, art. Given 10 minutes, you can think of 10 different ways to say or draw anything.

- **You think big, but you're also into the details.** Great creative work is absolutely in the details. Layouts need to be accurate for every medium an ad runs on. Choice of typeface and type size will make the difference between a good ad and a great one. Missing the placement of a registered trademark can be a disaster. You are full of big ideas but also devote the countless hours necessary to make sure your work is absolutely perfect.

- **You graciously accept direction and critique.** You are in the business of client service. Even though you are a creative genius, you must be able to accept criticism from people who know far less than you do about the creative process. There are times when you will have to gently persuade a client that their idea is wrong, and there are times when you have to swallow your pride, accept that your client will never let go of his love for hideous neon orange, and make it work to the best of your ability.

- **For you, no project is a small project.** You would love to create a Super Bowl ad, but you'll get the same satisfaction writing a credit card pitch letter. Sure, you're a little jealous of the guy sitting next to you who gets to work on a video shoot with Catherine Zeta-Jones, but you realize that the brochure you're creating is very important to your client. A good creative team will approach every project with an equal amount of respect and creativity.

66 Advertising is no place for oversize or fragile egos. Deadlines are real and fixed, with no regard to your personal life or the state of your muse. If you have the flu, and the client rejected all the previously presented work because he wanted to see something 'fresher but less clever,' and the deadline for materials is next week, and a radio in the next office is blaring music you hate—guess what? You either deliver a creative product on time or find another line of work. Of course, sometimes there's nothing like pressure to get the creative juices flowing."

—**John Kuraoka,** Freelance Copywriter

The Workplace

The creative team sits in the fun, social area, the place to show off to guests and clients. While the account management section may look like the typical corporate cubicle environment, the creative department area will usually have bright colors, cool furniture, and extras like pool tables or pinball machines (to get those creative juices flowing, of course!). And creatives who love their jobs often go the extra mile, so it wouldn't be surprising to see an art director working on a travel brochure about Italy getting into the spirit by filling the department with the buoyant strains of *Rigoletto*.

Where account executives usually work with a single client, creatives typically work for multiple clients simultaneously. This means that every day brings with it deadlines and a barrage of messages or phone calls from account executives who have no idea about the other 15 projects you're working on. Hours can be long, especially as deadlines for major projects loom. However, there is a degree of independence when it comes to the actual work you are producing, and the grueling commitment is balanced by the flexibility of working from home, or even a café, on a regular basis. Of course, those with more gregarious personalities will enjoy the social office space.

Creative roles require technical expertise and skills developed on the job. Background and experience vary within each position; consequently, the age range is wider than it is on the account management teams. Creatives also vary widely in personality and individual style. Different clients, brands, and projects demand different kinds of people. The type of person who creates a campaign for Folgers Coffee might be quite different from the one pegged for P. Diddy's latest energy drink.

"It's Comcastic"

Creativity is not an exact science, as demonstrated by Goodby, Silverstein & Partners' "Comcastic" Comcast campaign, which won *Adweek*'s award for best campaign in 2005 for the "breadth and depth of the creative." The campaign was the first attempt by the communications and cable service giant to create a nationwide image, and Goodby went through an exhaustive and competitive pitch process to win the $50 million account. The signature tagline "It's Comcastic" was actually a joke tossed out by co-creative director Jamie Barrett in an agency meeting. One memorable TV spot, featuring overdubbed archival footage from an old *$20,000 Pyramid* game show, was voiced by Mark Wenneker, Goodby's other creative director, who read the lines for the pitch version and proved to be the right fit when it came time to tape. It just goes to show: There's always a bit of luck that goes along with the months of rigorous planning and hard work.

The Salaries

Creative roles require some technical skills going in. Copywriters need solid writing skills, and art directors need training in the visual or graphic arts and a portfolio of work to showcase their experience. As a result, the job pays more than account management: $38,000 to $42,000 for a junior-level position and $45,000 or more if you have experience. However, creative roles are scarcer, and the competition for jobs is more intense.

Pay is typically commensurate with past achievement, often with additional money for those who have degrees and accolades from accredited design schools or writing programs. Creatives who are willing to relocate may get a slightly higher entry-level salary to compensate. Salaries rise quickly as creatives move up the ladder and work on more high-profile projects, with creative directors at top firms making as much as $200,000.

Prospects

True entry-level jobs on a creative team are hard to come by. Although some agencies have junior apprenticeship roles, many require a full portfolio and past experience to get in the door. As you break into the industry, you may want to consider taking a long-term freelance gig for an hourly wage to catch up. Once you prove yourself, you can secure a full-time position and move up to the bigger money and more prestigious clients.

It is possible to get an entry-level creative job if you have the skills and persistence, but these jobs are few and far between. You will definitely need a portfolio (your "book") to show that you know how to develop a concept, write advertising copy, or create visually stimulating and effective work.

If you don't have a full portfolio or relevant degree, consider starting off at a lesser-known company or a startup to gain that all-valuable experience. But if you have your heart set on a top-10 agency, you may find it easier to start off in account management or media to get your foot in the door and then cross over into the creative department once you get your book together.

Job Titles

As opposed to the standard hierarchy of the typical account management department, many creative departments are structured laterally, with several art directors and copywriters working on different brands and reporting to the same creative director. A typical team working on a given campaign will include an art director and copywriter, assisted by a junior art director and copywriter. Here are some of the more common titles, though not all will exist at every agency.

- **Creative Director**
  This is the head honcho of the creative department, reporting to agency brass and working closely with other agency execs. She is ultimately responsible for all creative work on campaigns designed by her the agency. She accepts any creative awards, sometimes alongside the writer and art director, on the company's behalf.

- **Senior Art Director/Senior Copywriter**
  This mid-level position reports directly to the creative director and oversees the work of several art directors or copywriters. He is also involved with the concepting and creative development for the largest and most high-profile ad campaigns. This job title is more likely to exist in a large agency.

- **Art Director**
  This person reports to either a senior art director or creative director, depending on the size of the department. He works directly with a copywriter to develop the concept and storyline for an ad campaign and creates the layout and compelling visuals. He is in frequent contact with the account manager and the account executive to develop and maintain the overall vision for a project. He may be asked to accompany the account management team on presentations to the client and answer any questions regarding the concept. He's also responsible for relaying to the creative team any subsequent revisions based on those meetings.

- **Copywriter**
  Again, depending on the size of the department, a copywriter reports either to a senior copywriter or directly to the creative

director. She works closely with the art director to develop a concept and is responsible for the words or scripts for an ad campaign. She might write anything from 30-second TV commercial dialogues to one-sentence print ads to text-heavy brochures. She may also be asked to accompany the account team to client meetings, especially if she and the art director are working closely on a complicated, high-profile project.

- **Junior Art Director**

    This entry-level person reports to one or more art directors. He does simple graphic design, preps for presentations, provides onsite assistance at photo or video shoots, and communicates with freelance photographers, directors, and other for-hire workers. The position of junior art director exists almost exclusively in the larger, full-service ad agencies.

- **Junior Copywriter**

    This entry-level person reports to one or more copywriters. She proofreads and writes some copy for smaller projects. She may work on one or many brands and may be called in for internal agency projects such as company newsletters or signs for company-wide meetings. The position of junior copywriter exists almost exclusively in the larger, full-service ad agencies.

Help, I didn't go to design school!

Many advertising agencies recruit heavily from design schools for their entry-level art director positions (for instance, Manhattan ad agencies recruit at Parsons or the School of Visual Arts). If your portfolio or writing samples are outstanding, an agency won't look down on you for attending a liberal arts school. Still, you might miss out on the networking and job gossip that go along with attending a feeder design school. If you're not at a design school, consider taking an evening or summer class at one to utilize their network and get their name on your résumé.

Freelancing

Freelancing is an enticing option, particularly for creative positions. It gives you the chance to gain some experience, make some contacts, and decide whether this really is what you want to do. Here are some of the benefits and drawbacks.

The benefits:

- You choose your work.

- Your commitment is short-term.

- You can work on a lot of different accounts and clients.

- You approach each project with a fresh perspective.

- You have full creative license and can take all the credit for your brilliant ideas.

- You are your own boss.

- You can structure your day as you wish.

- According to the U.S. Department of Labor's *Occupational Outlook Handbook*, writers and graphic artists are in demand.

The drawbacks:

- You don't have a regular source of income.

- You don't have the benefits of full-time employment: healthcare, 401(k), stock options, etc.

- Because clients like continuity, your lack of familiarity with an account may be held against you and your work.

- Your assignments can be lower profile than those of your agency counterparts.

- You're in a competitive market.

- You are your own administrative assistant.

The Ground Floor

Yes, we know that everyone has told you that you're the best artist ever and that you've been producing killer television commercials for your college station for the past two years. Unfortunately, that doesn't mean that you'll be able to start producing prime-time commercials right away. Recent college grads will likely start as freelancers, full-time interns, or junior art directors or copywriters.

An entry-level creative reports directly to one art director or copywriter but helps many people on the team. To gain experience, they may work on less exciting projects such as direct-mail postcards or human resources recruiting material. They also help mount designs onto boards for presentations, conduct background research for concepts, or do basic things such as inserting logos, fixing typos, and updating templates. New creatives may be called on to help out with internal company projects, such as company newsletters, posters or signs for around the office, or company announcements. And while there's not much contact with clients or agency execs, new creatives often work closely with their entry-level counterparts on the account management team.

During this time, it's wise to involve yourself in many creative projects, no matter how small. Assist in brainstorming sessions. Come up with your own ideas after hours and then pitch them to people on your team. Build up your portfolio with agency work or independent projects. Prove that you're capable of magnificent work and when it comes time for a promotion, people will think of you first.

66 Working at a big place is exciting, and it's a great way to network with really powerful people in the industry. But especially if you're a creative person, you might want to give some careful thought to starting out at a small place, where it's more likely that your input will be ultimately presented to the client. Even though I work at a very small agency, around 15 people, I've had the chance to work on some really big projects for really big brands, and the stuff that the clients—and ultimately the consumers—read is stuff that I actually wrote."

—**Catherine Sheehan,** Copywriter
Captains of Industry

MEDIA SERVICES

In a perfect world, ads would reach only those people who are open to buying the product. The media team works hard to approximate that perfect world. By doing extensive research, it tries to reduce the chance that the ad will be seen by people who have no interest in the product or service—which wastes the client's money—and increase the chance that likely customers will be exposed to the campaign.

A case of brilliance

In 2001 Guinness made its first foray into bottled beer in the company's 200-year history. But this new venture was complicated by the fact that for those 200 years, Guinness had branded itself on the principle that the "Perfect Pint" could only come from the tap. How could they maintain integrity with the loyal pub-going consumer while also convincing a fresh out-of-the-pub market that bottled Guinness was just as authentic as the original? It wasn't easy. When they first launched the new Guinness bottles, sales were disappointing. The public didn't go for it.

Enter BBDO New York, whose award-winning "Brilliant!" Guinness ads comically claim that the new bottled beverage is a breakthrough on par with other groundbreaking inventions, such as the telephone and suntan lotion. But coming up with the ad was only part of the equation. Media services needed to identify the key audience—in this case, sports viewers—and firmly position Guinness in this niche by, for instance, buying ad space during televised NFL games and sponsoring the hit ESPN show *Pardon the Interruption*, claiming exclusive beer advertising rights in the process. The result: a union of creative production and media services smarts that led to a 12.1 percent increase in bottled Guinness sales and a lift in sales on all Guinness products in 2005.

Media roles in advertising fall into two categories: media planning and media buying.

- **Media planners** conduct research and analysis to determine the target market and how best to reach it.

- **Media buyers** arrange for the ads to run in specific magazines, television shows, websites, billboards, and so on.

If you're creating a campaign for a brand of soda directed at the teen market, the media planner will hone in on the trends and interests for the target demographic, and the media buyer gets the ad placed where teen eyes are likely to catch it.

Personality Profile

Those who succeed in media services prefer to work on the research end of advertising. To see if you might make a good media planner or buyer, check out the following list of traits.

- **You're on top of all the trends.** You're the person who always knows about the coolest restaurants, websites, and gadgets months before everyone else does. Your friends call you to find out what's new and hip. Clients count on their media staff to be one step ahead of the game, and they want to work with people like you, who know about the hottest television shows and Internet sites before the competition does.

- **You're personable but not a pushover.** You're affable and people tend to like you, but even more important you're intelligent and savvy. You control your client's purse, which means that every single media outlet—and we do mean every single one—will be knocking on your door within moments of getting your business card. You can quickly assess which magazines, programs, and websites are the real deal and which ones are a real waste of time.

- **You're a negotiating machine.** Along with your people skills, you have keen intuition and serious negotiating chops. It's your responsibility to negotiate for the most effective ad space within your client's budget. You have great instincts, know when an asking price is too high, and can persuade vendors to meet your needs.

- **Your eyes are always open.** You're a pop culture aficionado. You soak it all in, down to watching shows and checking out websites that you don't love just to stay on top of the trends. Your clients count on you to identify what's hot, know their target audience, and place their ads in the best-possible locations. In some instances, you may control hundreds of thousands of your client's marketing dollars. Your clients trust you to spend that money wisely.

The Workplace

Media departments usually have a hip, chic look and feel that reflects their awareness of what's trendy and cool. But before you start thinking about how you're going to feng shui your office, you should know that as an entry-level employee, you'll probably be stuck in a cube. Don't worry, though: As soon as you get promoted, you can hand it off to the next unsuspecting college grad.

Media services is one of the most exciting departments to work in. Your day will be fast-paced, frenetic, and full of meetings. People trying to persuade you to put your client's ad in their magazine or website will show up, often unannounced, at your door. Your evenings may be consumed with research and analysis as you determine consumer habits relating to online music sharing. You'll learn about a ton of companies that you never knew existed and will establish great relationships with some of them. You will be wined, dined, and invited to some of the best parties in the biz. And it's truly rewarding to see your client's ad prominently displayed in the perfect magazine and know that it's there because of you.

In the past, while the account management and creative teams worked closely together, the media team tended to be more independent. The media director would work with the account director and the client to plan the overall strategy and goals for the campaign, but the media team would typically step in after the campaign has been created or neared completion, and their conversations with the client would be separate from other client-to-agency communication.

As interactive outlets continue to reshape the landscape, media planning finds itself increasingly involved in the early phases of a campaign's development. This trend seems likely to continue as the lines between different media components are further blurred, meaning media services will be a more integral part of the constant communications between clients and the different agency teams.

Big-budget media companies have been known to take media buyers at the hottest agencies on expenses-paid trips to Sundance, Fashion Week in Paris, or even the Olympic Games.

The Salaries

Entry-level media buyers can expect to earn $25,000 to $28,000 on the low end and $30,000 to $32,000 on the high end. For media planners, although an MBA is not necessary, coursework in communications marketing, business, or psychology or a few years of previous experience in the advertising industry is usually required. Consequently, salaries in this area tend to be higher. As a junior media planner, you can expect to make $30,000 to $38,000.

Like account management, media departments have a great deal of turnover. People often get raises by jumping to different agencies rather than waiting for promotions. High turnover means lots of open jobs. Proven experience and dedication will make you an appealing candidate for an entry-level job. If you have an internship on your résumé and voice a commitment to staying at the company for a significant amount of time, you might command a higher salary offer.

Prospects

Media services offers a wide variety of prospects for entry-level professionals, depending on educational background. Media planning positions typically ask for a bachelor's degree or coursework in communications, marketing, business, or psychology, plus some prior experience in the industry. Media buying, in contrast, is popular among recent college grads with no specialized experience. If you are persistent and able to promote yourself as an imaginative, trendsetting, and analytical person, you have a good chance of securing an entry-level media role.

Media outlets for advertising used to consist entirely of radio, television, magazines, and newspapers, but the market is changing rapidly as new technologies emerge. Advertisers are increasingly looking to emerging forms of media: online, mobile, social networks, blogs, podcasts, and more. It is now possible to place an ad in literally thousands of locations, and advertisers need media professionals who understand new technologies and embrace fresh challenges. There will always be openings for people with this specialized knowledge.

If you are a fast learner, an effective campaign planner, and a skilled negotiator, you will move up quickly from your entry-level job. Clients want results, and if you have a hand in delivering them and don't spend *all* your time at industry parties, you can expect your first promotion in a year to a year and a half. As you climb the ladder, you'll manage larger budgets, handle multiple clients, and work with major new businesses.

Job Titles

Here are the roles that exist in most media departments.

- **Media Director**

  This senior person reports to the agency higher-ups. He oversees the media supervisors and bears responsibility for all of the work done by his department. He may also be called on to run the **media plan** if the agency wins a large account for a new client.

- **Media Supervisor**

  The media supervisor reports to the media director and manages the work of several buyers and planners within the department. She is in close and frequent contact with the account manager and the client, managing larger client budgets and helping make strategic decisions regarding a campaign.

- **Media Buyer**

  The media buyer reports to the media supervisor. He negotiates with sales reps from various media outlets to buy and place ads targeted by the media planner. He is the wheeler-and-dealer, acquiring media space in the most time-effective and cost-efficient way possible. He works with a variety of media types, unless his team specializes in a particular aspect of interactive media (only at the larger full-service agencies or specialized agencies).

- **Media Planner**

  The media planner also reports to the media supervisor. She researches the public's viewing and media habits to determine where and when an ad will run. She is in frequent contact with the media buyer, since her decisions help guide the media plan and buying process. Her role is numbers oriented and heavy on research and analysis. Some media planners have direct contact with account managers or clients; others do not.

A **media plan** details the budget, media outlets, dates, and times related to the components of a particular campaign launch.

- **Junior Media Buyer** (also known as **Assistant Media Buyer**)
  This entry-level person assists the media buyer with a fair amount of number crunching and budget tracking. He keeps track of where and when client ads are running and does some basic negotiating.

- **Assistant Media Planner**
  This entry-level person assists the media planner. She does lots of research and simple number crunching and spends a lot of time with PowerPoint and Excel.

The Ground Floor

As a recent college grad in media services, you will work with different products, companies, and media outlets on your way to an expertise in brand researching and placement price haggling. No two days will be the same. You'll work at a fast pace and learn a lot very quickly.

During the day, media planners spend a lot of time researching the client's brand or reading up on the latest media developments. PowerPoint presentations and Excel spreadsheets are the tools of the trade, which means that if you're not already proficient in those programs when you begin, you'll become a whiz soon enough. After a few months on the job, media planners will become responsible for their own research projects, and media buyers will attend meetings where media outlets will woo them in the hopes of getting their client's business.

In the beginning the hours will be long and the salaries low, but the perks begin immediately. Recent grads admit that the media parties, holiday gifts, fancy dinners, and tickets to sporting events and concerts make all the hard work worthwhile. Your friends might be annoyed when you blow them off to stay late at the office, but they'll probably forgive you when you get them into a club where Lindsay Lohan is hanging out in the VIP section.

Media services is all about on-the-job training. You'll gain experience with research and brand strategy, expert knowledge of the newest forms of media out there, and the know-how to approach a revenue spreadsheet in a smart and cost-efficient way. You'll also meet tons of people, so if you're good at networking, you will find yourself with lots of useful contacts. A job in media is a terrific break-in role for a recent college grad who is light on experience but interested in the industry. Media jobs provide opportunities for growth and development and look great on your résumé if you decide to go in a different direction.

66 I find it rewarding to be able to actually view what you do. You work hard to create a plan and implement it, then you see the fruits of your labor when you turn on the TV like millions of other people. I was looking for a job that allowed me to use both business sense and creative impulses together in an industry that I enjoy. I *am* a viewer and a reader and have strong opinions about what I experience. Those opinions are utilized and taken advantage of in what I do every day."

—Erica Slomak, National Broadcast Negotiator
MindShare

OTHER AREAS OF INTEREST

Not everyone fits neatly into an account, creative, or media category. If you're still searching for the perfect role in the advertising industry, you may want to explore a few additional areas.

Production

Production is one of the most crucial aspects of the ad creation process, yet most people outside the industry are barely aware of it. After the creative team designs the ad campaign and writes the copy, it's the production team that turns the pretty computer graphic into a magazine ad, direct-mail piece, billboard, or all of the above.

Many of the largest advertising companies have an in-house production team to work on broadcast production for television and radio commercials or print production for magazines, newspapers, brochures, and more. Sometimes, an agency's in-house production team will handle only one type of production (such as print production on pieces that are 10 pages at most) and they'll outsource broadcast production or large-scale print production to a specialized firm. The agency's production team works closely with outside vendors—directors, film production companies, and editors, for example—to ensure that a high-quality piece is produced.

The production team also works closely with the creative team to make sure that the creative team's concepts can actually be implemented. In fact, most production teams like to sit down with the creative and account management teams before an idea is presented to the client. That way the production manager can point out if a graphic won't be visible in a particular medium, if a thicker card stock might look more elegant, or if a particular director would be perfect for this ad. Throughout the creative stages, production is called on to reference sample books of materials, colors, paper styles, and more. The most successful production people are very creative in addition to possessing excellent administrative, technical, and organizational skills.

Traffic

A high-profile ad campaign may have as many as 20 people working on it, and if their efforts are not coordinated, disaster ensues. An agency working on a direct-mail catalog may need to create a 50-page book, an envelope, a letter, and a coupon. Mary from accounts has the envelope and the letter, but where is the book that had all of the comments from proofreading in the margins? Joe from creative claims that he passed it off to Terry in production. But Terry can't find it and thought that Mary had taken it off her desk to review. What a nightmare!

Most full-service agencies have an entire department devoted to managing the logistics and scheduling of these massive projects. A traffic coordinator/project manager keeps track of the materials, shuffling pieces of the campaign between account management, the creatives, and production. He knows who is working on what piece and when and who is reviewing what piece and when. He also keeps track of all the drafts and discarded versions in case someone chooses to go back to something done previously. He ensures that no piece goes into final production before everyone has given final approval. In some cases, the traffic coordinator may also be responsible for maintaining and updating the production schedule.

The traffic department is a great place for entry-level prospects to get their foot in the door. Although they don't have direct client contact, they are crucial to the successful navigation of a project and are connected to every department within the company. In addition, others in an agency will cozy up to traffickers for those occasions when a project needs to cut to the head of the production queue.

New Business

When word gets out that a top brand is looking for a new advertising agency, many agencies will jump in to compete. At any given time, an agency is likely involved in one or more new business pitches. Enter the new business team.

The new business team decides which open accounts are worth pursuing. They assess the internal resources needed for a pitch, pull in any volunteers from other departments to assist, and then work day and night, using the best creative minds and killer materials to win over the prospective client.

New business work involves creativity, dynamic presentation skills, and the ability to work on many different pitches at once. It's a high-profile role, since the agency's executive team counts on new business to boost revenue. As someone in new business, you will work long hours, and your work will be scrutinized closely. Your job will be stressful, but also exhilarating.

66 You can always tell when someone is on new business by the growing pile of napkins, ketchup packets, and takeout menus hastily pushed aside on their desk. New business is a whirlwind that's incredibly challenging and incredibly rewarding. Your head feels like it may explode after a 14-hour day of moderating focus groups with consumers, researching and analyzing the competition's strategy, and participating in hours upon hours of brainstorming sessions. But because it's so collaborative you remain energized by the team around you and your shared goal of winning!"

—**Radhika Dewan,** Account Planner
Ogilvy & Mather

Research and Analysis

In addition to the media planners, some advertising companies have a department fully dedicated to research and consumer insight. This department gives senior decision makers within the agency the detailed information and analysis they need to have strategic discussions and provide advertising and marketing solutions to their clients. People in research and analysis may analyze general media trends or report on how the agency measures up against its competitors. They help out with research and data for new business pitches, top clients, and larger campaigns. People in these departments tend to have an analytical bent. Many have advanced degrees in statistics or math, as well as core competency with research software and data programs.

More and more companies are seeing the value of detailed market research, which makes for good career prospects in this department over the coming years. If you love numbers and data and want to approach the advertising industry from the analytical side, a research analyst position could be a terrific position for you.

Strategic Planning

Strategic planning is charged with informing the creative side by clearly defining a market and helping to shape the client's goals. On rare occasions, these people will exist as a separate department, though in most agencies they are a subgroup or function, depending on the agency size, of research and analysis. They are often assigned to specific brands or products and maintain a close watch on what target consumers do and what they need. For instance, if you work on the strategic planning group whose client manufactures Brand X jeans, through your focus groups, surveys, and observations, you might find that women tend to keep a good pair of jeans for years. With this insight, the creative team could craft a campaign emphasizing that Brand X jeans are durable and comfortable. Strategic planning is often brought in to assist in new business, suggesting ways that an agency may tackle a particular pitch to a new client.

THE CAREER GENIE

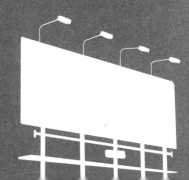

The Career Genie looks into his crystal ball to predict the career fortunes of six eager job seekers. What does the future hold for you? Compare yourself to these brave young souls.

~~~~~~

Susie

SNAPSHOT

At 21, Susie is the life of the party. She makes a great first impression with everyone she meets, and her network of friends would rival the CEO of Omnicom's. Though not necessarily a straight-A student, her energy and her "Go team!" attitude is enough to get fellow students clamoring to work with her on group projects. Friends say she should run for student government, but she's too busy as business manager for her dance troupe and star of the intramural volleyball team. She's spent the last three summer breaks working at her parents' jewelry store back home and even created their website. A senior sociology major at a small liberal arts college, Susie had figured on a career in nonprofit until she spoke with someone from an ad agency at her school's career fair. The opportunity to manage projects in a fast-paced, cutting-edge environment held an instant appeal. She's now turning her sights toward advertising.

OUTLOOK

Susie should focus her efforts on finding a position as an assistant account executive. Her strong personality and good people skills would be a tremendous asset with clients and other departments. She has ample experience working with teams, and someone with her energy and attitude is always in demand for account management. A less-than-stellar GPA shouldn't hurt her if Susie stresses the leadership and organizational skills she developed as business manager of her dance troupe. In an interview, she should focus on her teamwork and discuss some successful team projects and her role in them. Susie doesn't have internship experience, but she can spin her work at her parents' store as a training ground in consumer and client relations.

Vince

SNAPSHOT

Vince has always had an entrepreneurial spirit—even as a kid, whether it was selling chocolate bars in elementary school or managing his lawn care business in his teens. He enjoyed finding creative ways to promote his endeavors as much as the jobs themselves. After high school, he decided to buffer his enterprising spirit with some sound knowledge. He excelled in his studies, and as a junior heading for an economics degree at UPenn, he landed a coveted summer internship at a prestigious investment banking firm in New York. He hated it. Sitting at a desk all day working on projects that were dull and uninspiring left him completely disillusioned. Coming back for his senior year, he stuck with his intended major, since he enjoyed the coursework. But directionless after graduation, he took a job as an analyst at a credit card company, mostly just to collect a paycheck. Vince occasionally dabbled in web design, and one day a friend asked for his help putting together a website for his band. Vince was amazed at how much he enjoyed the experience of promoting someone else. He signed up for an evening graphic design class at a local technical college to learn more. Now 23, he's considering what careers may be available if he decides to keep pursuing this.

OUTLOOK

Vince should look into a junior art director position at an agency. He has an affinity for web design and promotion, and his personal design projects have helped him develop the skills necessary to be a successful art director in the future. His interest in advertising is relatively recent, but if he can use his graphic design coursework to build up a portfolio, he should at least be able to get some interviews. His work in economics and business won't be held against him, particularly because he can point to some real accomplishments and accolades in this field, but he'll need to display a genuine commitment to advertising in his interviews. When applying, he should put together a collection of his works that showcases the depth and breadth of his ability, including both print and web design. It would also help him to include a letter of recommendation from one of his graphic design instructors.

Lani

SNAPSHOT

Lani's parents always said she'd grow up to be a doctor. As a child, she used to take in sick animals and nurse them back to health, or at least try to. She actually enjoyed going to the doctor's office, and when she was there, she would ask him questions that displayed an impressive understanding for someone her age. In high school, instead of reading *Teen Vogue* or *Cosmo,* she was reading her parents' *Prevention* and *Good Medicine* magazines, and she spent her weekends volunteering at the children's hospital. But when it came time to head off to college, she didn't opt for the premed path. Instead, she chose a double major in biology and business, splitting her time between the lab and product research and management. During the summers, she interned in the marketing department of a large pharmaceutical company, and after graduation she took a job as a junior account executive there. After two years, the size and anonymity have begun to wear on her. At 24, she's looking for a change of scenery.

OUTLOOK

Lani would do well to check into options at a specialized agency in the healthcare industry. Her degree in biology and her marketing work in pharmaceuticals gives her knowledge of the products from both a professional and a consumer perspective. This is exactly the kind of background such an agency looks for. She should have no problem fashioning a résumé that clearly displays her qualifications, which her current supervisors can corroborate with good references. She could pursue either account management or media planning or even copywriting, depending on the amount of medical writing she has done. Specialized agencies are in a competitive market, so she'll have to really operate her network to find out where the jobs are opening and get in there fast.

Luke

SNAPSHOT

Luke, 20, is an English major with a love for the written word that started before he could read. The satisfaction he gets from grinding out a solid essay or short story goes way beyond grades or accolades. As co-founder and lead writer/editor for a student-run travel magazine, he's had the opportunity to visit colleges in other cities and states and has even taken his talents overseas when he spent a semester in Finland. He discovered a particular aptitude for composing short, witty descriptions of everything from local food and music to styles of dress and speech. After graduation, a small publishing house offered to publish some of the travel mag's work. Luke assumed full-time editor duties collecting and preparing some of the travel writings for publication, a job that frequently required 60-plus hours of work a week. With that project wrapping up, he's exploring where he can next turn his energy and talents.

OUTLOOK

Luke would be a tremendous asset as a junior copywriter. Although not directly related to advertising, his experiences writing travel pieces have sharpened his ability to compose in the succinct, catchy tone that agencies are looking for. His editing experience further trained him for the meticulous attention to detail he'll need in this field. The fact that he's had some professional publishing experience provides an extra boost to his portfolio. When applying for a copywriting job, he should include different samples of his work: short excerpts and articles from the travel guides, lengthier pieces he's done for class, and samples of work he's edited. He should also stress his ability to work well with a team and independently (while traveling) and any leadership skills he acquired in his role as editor.

Brooklyn

SNAPSHOT

Brooklyn, 19, always seems to be up on the latest trends—the hottest bands, most fashionable wear, and tickets to the most sought-after shows. She was the first to wear Uggs and the first to stop wearing them. Her notoriety as the go-to girl for what's happening when it's happening even extends into the blogosphere, where her semiregular "it girl" postings on a popular nightlife website have made her something of a local celebrity. It was this exposure that landed her a spot with a youth marketing firm as a "trendsetter," providing them with monthly reports on what's cool for college students. But beneath the fashionista exterior, Brooklyn's a good student who's moving into the senior year of her marketing major at a fairly competitive school with a solid 3.00. She has aspirations to work at a marketing or advertising firm post-graduation.

OUTLOOK

Brooklyn could catwalk into an entry-level position in media planning. Her proven trend savviness will make her very attractive to an agency looking to help clients reach young audiences. Her knack for finding and communicating what's up-and-coming is a good tool not just for research, but for ad placement as well, since Brooklyn will always know which new magazines and websites will reach a trend-hungry youth audience. Her marketing major is a good indication to potential employers that she knows the field, which is crucial given her lack of interning or office experience. She may want to take a course or two on statistics and analysis to demonstrate her ability to work with figures. When applying, she should stress her marketing background, professionally, personally, and academically. She should really play up her understanding of the 18- to 24-year-old audience and point out instances where she's used that knowledge to the direct benefit of clients. And since she's coming from a notable school, she should start working her career services and alumni centers as soon as possible to get information and make connections.

Paul

SNAPSHOT

Paul is a technology fiend. He's a certified computer geek with a strong visual sense and an intelligent programming mind. Too restless for the classroom and too advanced to really learn much for his money, he left school after picking up his associate degree in computer science. He's spent the last five years as a freelancer doing both graphic design work and interactive online programming. His "Gearhead's Corner" blog, covering all things techie, has garnered him a reasonable following on the web and has been a great way to pick up work. In the past he's taught entry-level computer classes, but he quit when the lack of flexibility cut into his band's touring schedule—he plays bass. Now he's 27 and reaching the point in his life when the stability of a full-time gig holds more appeal than the open road. He's done freelance work for advertising agencies in the past and feels his imagination would get the best workout there.

OUTLOOK

Paul should definitely consider exploring a creative position. His limited advertising background and lack of print and broadcast experience might hurt his chances at a large full-service agency. But his ample freelance work and strong background in design and programming might be good enough to start as an art director at an agency specializing in interactive advertising. He brings a great deal of creativity and know-how to the table and could create effective and engaging online ads that display a true understanding of the user experience. The looser setting of a smaller specialized agency or boutique may also be a better fit for his freewheeling attitude. But Paul's got one major hurdle to overcome no matter where he focuses his energies: He's been out of school for some time and the few jobs he's done in advertising haven't netted him a long list of contacts. If he wants to break in, he'll need to get his name out there by attending industry events, amping up his freelance ad work, and networking wherever he can. He should also try to expand his portfolio beyond web design if he wants to be marketable to a full-service agency.

PART II: HOW TO BREAK IN

3

PREPARING YOURSELF FOR THE JOB SEARCH

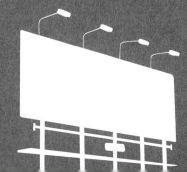

What really drives you? Do you love working with people? Are you passionate about design? Do you enjoy doing research? The following sections outline the skills that aspiring creative, account, and media services gurus need to stand out. As you read, assess yourself as a candidate. How closely do the skills presented match with your experiences and inclinations? There's no need to freak out if you're on the verge of graduation and don't have the qualities or background described here. We'll give you a few tips on how to gain experience in these areas—and how to gain it fairly quickly, if need be. And we'll help you put together a résumé that shows off what a great candidate you already are.

IDENTIFY KEY ACCOUNT EXECUTIVE SKILLS

Account management is all about service. As an account manager, you need to make sure that everyone is happy—your clients, the creative team, your boss—while simultaneously managing the entire campaign process and making sure that the end result is something that the client loves and that makes you proud. Applicants for account management positions don't need the technical skills and prerequisite knowledge that their creative counterparts do, since most important account management skills are learned on the job. Instead, they need to demonstrate that they are articulate, personable, and organized.

- **Effective communication skills:** Working in advertising can sometimes be seen as battle of wills, and account managers are often the refs. It's your job to take a client's vague idea and articulate it so clearly and concisely that the creative team immediately knows what to do. You'll also be the one to convey bad news to the client in a tactful way and give criticism to the creative team without ruffling feathers. You need to pitch ideas in a compelling way and not crumble when the clients or creatives try to twist your arm. Through it all, you'll need to keep a level of passion and enthusiasm that keeps everyone motivated.

- **Presentation skills:** In addition to interpersonal tact, account management also requires that you develop your formal communication skills. At the beginning of your career, you probably won't be the one leading the pitch, but a prospective employer will want to know that when the time comes, you'll be able to stand up and present to a client with confidence. Training programs such as Toastmasters can help you hone your speaking skills. Your résumé should highlight any leadership positions you have had and any events where you have given a presentation or speech. Participation in student government, theatrical performances, and public-speaking courses are great ways to demonstrate comfort and ease in front of an audience.

    Toastmasters is an organization whose members work on developing communication and leadership skills (toastmasters.org). Most clubs are made up of 20 to 30 people who practice making speeches each week.

- **A leader's mentality:** As an account executive, you bear the responsibility to keep things moving and people happy. Good leaders rarely take full credit and often take an inordinate amount of blame. Demonstrate your leadership ability by highlighting successful group projects at school, concerts or plays you've helped put on, or experience on any team.

- **A strong work ethic:** It stinks to be at work late, night after night, under stressful conditions. But advertising often calls for this kind of dedication. In your interview, demonstrate your willingness to work hard by providing examples of your persistence on projects that took an enormous time commitment.

- **An ability to perform under pressure:** When something goes wrong, you will need to think on your feet, come up with a solution, and explain the situation in a way that gives people confidence in your decisions. Nothing is ever perfect, and even if you have a handle on all aspects of a project, things will still go wrong that might upset your client. If you can gracefully handle little pitfalls such as a missed deadline or a color match error, your client will walk away thinking more highly of you than if everything had gone smoothly. In an interview, mention times when you've been resourceful in handling a difficult problem.

- **A methodical nature:** You will be expected to keep close track of your projects, attend every meeting and conference call, and manage deadlines for the creative team. Demonstrate your methodical nature by coming prepared for your interview with clean copies of your résumé and any other relevant material. Make sure your briefcase or bag is orderly. Dress neatly. Don't appear disheveled or flustered. These little gestures go a long way toward demonstrating that you are organized and responsible enough to handle the job.

66 I was working on a pitch for an old coffee company that was trying to become more relevant among younger business professionals. In the meeting, the head of the department asked, 'I heard that Starbucks took out a big spread in *BusinessWeek* magazine. Has anyone seen it?' On a fluke of good fortune, I had seen the magazine that morning and had torn out the ad to bring in. To everyone in that meeting, it looked like I was super up on the competition ALL the time! My boss was thrilled, and I vowed to read every magazine cover to cover and always keep up with competitive info from then on!"

—**Marissa Levick,** former Account Executive

- **Proficiency in proofreading:** If your work includes typos and simple errors, you and your team look unpolished and unprofessional. Proofreading may not be part of your job description (in fact, many agencies have a dedicated proofreading department), but you are the last line of defense before materials go to the client and any errors automatically become your responsibility. There is nothing worse than sending over copy containing grammatical errors that could have easily been fixed with an extra 10 minutes of care. The same rule applies to your résumé and cover letter. Make sure they're clean and error free. Reread follow-up letters or thank-you notes several times before sending them.

- **An ability to multitask:** You must be able to multitask without compromising quality. Account executives balance many projects, each with moving parts and deadlines. If you've ever organized a major event, such as a formal dance, a play, or a charity concert, or if you've ever held a position as secretary in an organization, you'll want to place that experience front and center on your résumé.

Quick tips for boosting your résumé

If you want to prove that you enjoy working closely with people:

- Suggested coursework: List psychology and sociology courses, and courses with lots of group projects.

- Potential extracurriculars: Include Greek life, sports teams, student government, theater.

- Internships: List anything in which you've had to organize groups of people, such as a community service program or local politician's election campaign.

- Last-minute tips: Sign up for a graduation or social committee, plan an event or fund-raiser, volunteer.

IDENTIFY KEY CREATIVE SKILLS

Some departments in advertising allow you to learn on the job, but creative positions require a defined skill set before you walk through the door. This is true even at the entry level. To hit the ground running, you need previous design or writing experience. This doesn't mean that you need a degree from a premier design school or a master's in English lit, but you do need to show you have a creative flair and are tech savvy and a team player. To stand out in the field, you'll need the following skill sets.

- **The ability to generate ideas:** Some clients will give you a specific direction for what they want. Others will be vague, forcing you to inspire yourself. Either way, it's up to the creative team to come up with a powerful and original concept that communicates the product's goals and identity. Junior creatives are expected to bring a fresh quality to their work. From the start, you'll be given the opportunity to generate ideas for small projects and compete for the chance to work on bigger campaigns. It's fair to assume that a large percentage of your ideas will get shot down. When that happens, you'll need to store away those rejected ideas for the future and bounce right back with even more. You'll be hired based on your portfolio, so make sure it displays your range. Stand out in an interview by discussing instances when your ideas have generated revenue or accomplished goals for an organization or event.

- **Flexibility:** Flexibility is essential. In the same week, you may tackle an ad for a skateboarding company, a fast-food chain, and a bank, each with its own unique image, market, and branding. You will often have to create within the confines of someone else's preferences. Successful creatives can synthesize their personal style with the client's goals to create a compelling campaign. When discussing ad campaigns that have influenced you, try to demonstrate your range and diversity.

66 TV and print shoots may sound glamorous, but often they are long, hard, and boring. Even worse, when a cool shoot in some tropical locale does come up, your boss, who hasn't gone out on the field in months or even years, decides their skills will be needed on this one. I once got to go shoot an accountant at his 'office' in the suburbs. It turns out his 'small business' was really small—he actually ran it out of the basement of his father's law office. I found myself sipping on a lukewarm Coke in a dark, damp, cold basement. I thought the photographer was going to kill me as he begrudgingly tried to light the man's desk next to the hot water heater and a pile of old legal boxes."

—**Paul Fombelle,** Account Executive

- **Solid knowledge of the competition:** Are other companies using a celebrity spokesperson? A cartoon? A puppet? As the person responsible for the creative aspect of a campaign that will be seen by millions of people and cost the client a pretty penny, you need to be aware of the ads around you, especially those of the competition. Stay educated. Keep your eyes open and pay attention to *every* ad you see. Research the company you're interviewing with and arrive prepared to discuss competitive advertising campaigns and your perspective on them.

The One

A good creative knows what works and what doesn't, and one way to learn that is to keep an eye on award-winning creative work. The One Show is an annual award show hosted by the One Club for the best ads in print, radio, television, design, interactive, and new media. You can check out the winners on their website (oneclub.org) or in *The One Show Book.* The One Club, which also hosts programs and competitions for students, is a nonprofit organization of advertising creatives dedicated to nurturing the next generation of geniuses. It also publishes a quarterly magazine, *one. a magazine,* for the creative advertising community.

- **Proficiency in the latest software:** Knowledge of software design tools is no longer an added bonus; it is an absolute necessity. And if you are a younger person, older co-workers may look to you for guidance on the latest versions of design programs. If you need a refresher course (or a basic education) in design software, enroll in a summer or evening class. Luckily, you won't be required to demonstrate your Illustrator abilities during an interview, but if your portfolio doesn't display your prowess with common programs, you may be asked to go home, create a sample project, and present it the following day.

  On your résumé, mention all the computer programs in which you're proficient. And keep your list up-to-date!

- **Copywriting basics:** Pictures tell. Words sell. To get across a compelling message about a brand or product during a 30-second commercial or in a one-page magazine spot, you need good copywriting skills and the ability to generate powerful, persuasive words. In your interview, highlight experiences that demonstrate your ability to communicate successfully with an audience.

- **Basic production know-how:** A good creative is aware of the basic production needs for the various types of advertisements she is working with. The ability to visualize how fonts, colors, and layout will appear in print or on film will help shape ideas for a particular campaign. Any instances in which you've shown foresight in this area or have had to adjust to production limitations would be great to discuss in an interview.

- **A team-player attitude:** Advertising works on extremely tight deadlines and requires employees with flexibility, patience, and a can-do attitude. Are you willing to go the extra mile when necessary? Are you the kind of person who will take one for the team? If so, you should emphasize those attributes in your interview. Highlight your involvement on an athletic team, academic club, music group, or community service organization. Talk about situations in which you really went above and beyond the call of duty.

- **Effective communication skills:** The ability to articulate ideas clearly, both to clients and to other members of your team, is critical. Whether you are describing a creative concept to your art director or presenting a variety of potential campaign ideas to a client, it is imperative that you communicate effectively. And remember: A good communicator sometimes listens rather than talks! You should include any experience as a peer counselor, tutor, or team captain or any other leadership role in your résumé.

- **Willingness to accept criticism:** Inevitably, some of your great ideas will be rejected or changed almost beyond recognition. It can be frustrating to take direction from a client who knows a lot less about the creative process than you do, but you are in the business of serving. It's important to take suggestions with a smile and refine your concept so that it is both unique and a good fit with your client's goals. If you've ever been on a team, either athletic or academic, you've likely had to adjust to criticism. This flexibility would be good to discuss in an interview.

- **Knowledge of historic ad campaigns:** A solid knowledge of advertising history makes you a better creative. You'll be aware of what has been successful (or unsuccessful) in the past and will be able to use that knowledge to your client's advantage. Potential employers will ask you about your favorite ad campaigns—why you like them, and how you would improve them. Cultivate your knowledge by researching the notable campaigns created by the company you are interviewing with. If you've taken any classes that relate to media and advertising history, make sure to list them on your résumé.

Quick tips for boosting your résumé

If you want to prove that you love writing:

- Suggested coursework: List English, history, anything in the arts and humanities.

- Potential extracurriculars: Include student newspaper, travel guides, blogging.

- Last-minute tip: Write up promotional material for a local band or campus club.

If you want to prove that you love art and design:

- Suggested coursework: Include studio arts, graphic design, art history.

- Potential extacurriculars: List art, set/costume design, illustrations for a journal.

- Last-minute tip: Design promotional material for a local band or campus club.

IDENTIFY KEY MEDIA SERVICES SKILLS

People in media services make sure the right audience sees the right ads at the right time. Expert knowledge of myriad products and an awareness of what people of all ages and interests are watching, reading, and listening to are the hallmarks of a successful media services professional. If you can demonstrate analytical skills and ease with numbers, as well as a passion for media and pop culture, you will be a perfect fit for an entry-level media job.

- **Experience in research and analysis:** Creating the perfect media plan takes an expert knowledge of the market and competition. Need to figure out where to place a diaper ad? You may have to conduct focus groups with mothers of infants, analyze sales trends from the leaders in the diaper industry, and use research and reference tools to put together a detailed course of action. When organizing your résumé, highlight large research projects you've undertaken with a professor or on your own. Term papers or a senior thesis, grant proposals, or any internship experience that required you to do research or analysis will highlight your talent in this area.

- **Comfort with numbers:** Common tasks include calculating the return on an investment, determining costs per unit or click, and manipulating demographics. You must be at ease working with numbers and able to spot errors quickly. It's a good idea to freshen up with some introductory-level math and statistics courses. On your résumé, highlight relevant classes you've taken, especially if you've aced them!

- **Capacity to see the big picture:** It's easy to get caught up in all the numbers, details, and stats. However, it's important to approach each project from a broader strategic angle and keep in mind the client's desires for their product's image. Media plans need to focus on the target market, but they also have to include enough variety to reach that target market at many different **touch points.** And all this usually has to be done on a tight budget! In your résumé, focus on leadership positions you've held and the strategic decisions you've been involved with, as well as the results you've achieved.

Touch points are basically all the opportunities an ad has to reach the consumer, be it via television, radio, print, online, or in the street.

66 I think that the most pressure comes from having to perform in front of the client and respond immediately to their changing needs. This happened recently when I was testing different aspects of a marketing program in consumer focus groups. It had taken weeks to prepare the stimuli to show the focus group respondents, so it took me by surprise when after watching just one focus group, the client decided to approach the program from a completely different perspective. This basically meant that I had about 15 minutes to rewrite pages of concepts before the next focus group started!"

—**Radhika Dewan,** Account Planner
Ogilvy & Mather

- **Ability to form professional relationships:** When it comes to the cost of advertising, prices are often negotiable. Here's an example. Mary and Joe are media buyers. Both spend the same amount of money buying space for their clients' ads on a specific website. Joe gets exactly what he paid for. But the website companies like Mary so much that they bonus her some extra placements and bump her to a better slot for no extra cost. Mary's clients get more for their money and have a greater chance of being seen by the target audience. You could say this outcome is just luck, but Mary's success demonstrates the importance of good people skills and relationship building. Employers look for indications that you're more of a Mary than a Joe.

- **Networking smarts:** Attending industry parties and networking are key parts of the job. You'll go to events, talk to people, and learn as much as you can about different products and companies. The more contacts you have, the more valuable you'll be to your agency. Communicating with ease and listening effectively are crucial in establishing relationships with vendors, so demonstrate those abilities in your interview. If you've got contacts in advertising or media, it's okay to drop their names in an interview, but cap it at one or two, max! You want to portray yourself as well connected, not overbearing.

- **Open-minded enthusiasm:** In media services, it's not uncommon to find yourself working on a plan for a hot new Pepsi campaign with Beyoncé Knowles one day and an ad for a local bargain appliance store the next. You'll need to bring the same interest and intensity to all your projects. Your interviewer should come away feeling that you are open-minded and willing to put 100 percent of yourself into every project you work on.

- **Understanding of industry terms:** ROI, CPM, CRM . . . these are just a few of the abbreviations that will become a familiar part of your everyday discussions. Get to know these industry-specific terms before interviewing:

  - » **B2B:** Business to Business (transactions between businesses)
  - » **B2C:** Business to Consumer (transactions between a business and a consumer)
  - » **CPC:** Cost per Click (cost to an advertiser each time someone clicks on their Internet ad); also referred to as Pay per Click (PPC)
  - » **CPM:** Cost per Thousand (cost to reach every 1,000th person in your target market)
  - » **CRM:** Customer Relationship Management (efforts to increase customer satisfaction)
  - » **CTR:** Click-Through Rate (the percentage of total viewers who click on a specific ad)
  - » **ROI:** Return on Investment (money made as result of an ad)
  - » **ROS:** Run of Site (when an ad rotates evenly throughout every page on a website—this is cheaper than choosing specific pages to run on!)
  - » **SEO:** Search Engine Optimization (configuring your website to maximize the ranking on search engines, such as Google and Yahoo)

- **Solid negotiating ability:** Anyone who has ever been to a flea market knows that the first price is never the best price. Firm and tactful negotiating skills are a valuable asset for any successful media buyer. On your résumé, highlight jobs and experiences you have had that required negotiation on your part. Good negotiating also includes doing research so that you can make reasonable requests. Stress the business knowledge you have gained from research, coursework, or jobs.

- **Great organizational abilities:** Planners and buyers are working with lots of data. They need a system in place that helps them keep track of what they have scheduled, when campaigns are due to run, and what their recommendations are for a specific media buy. In your interview and on your résumé, stress your organizational strengths and your ability to keep track of multiple projects at the same time.

Quick tips for boosting your résumé

If you want to prove that you're fascinated with media:

- Suggested coursework: List media studies, psychology, marketing, advertising.

- Potential extracurriculars: Include theater, college radio, business/ marketing for a student group.

- Last-minute tip: Spend a summer doing media-related research or get a short-term media internship.

If you want to prove that you're numbers oriented:

- Suggested coursework: List economics, math, statistics.

- Potential extracurriculars: Include business or treasurer position in an organization.

- Internships: List anything in finance or mathematics.

- Last-minute tip: Get involved with a professor's research or tutor kids in math.

CRAFT A KILLER RÉSUMÉ

Now that you've assessed yourself as a candidate, it's time to take the skills you've identified and market yourself. The simple goal of a résumé is to get you an interview. Your résumé (or portfolio, if you're a creative) is your first, and sometimes only, opportunity to make an impression on a prospective employer. It is *the* opportunity to tell your story and convince someone that you can add value to his or her business.

Don't be afraid of the education and experience sections of a résumé. If you're still in school or are a recent grad, companies don't expect you to have an extensive background in advertising. As you're marketing yourself, focus on instances that required resourcefulness and creative problem solving. Your job as a waitress gave you terrific knowledge of the service industry (what do you think an advertising agency is?), and that babysitting gig taught you about responsibility. And don't underestimate the power of extracurricular activities.

Here are 10 basic tips on how to create a résumé that will get you noticed.

1. **Begin by writing an objective.** Some people begin their résumé by diving right into their education or work experience, but if there's not a lot of advertising in your background or if you're moving over from another industry, it's wise to begin by specifying the exact role you're looking for. The objective statement is an opportunity to clarify the area you want to work in, such as account management, creative, or media services. It can be as simple as, "Seeking an entry-level position in account management at a top advertising agency."

2. **Emphasize your strengths.** Create a focused presentation of yourself that relates to your proven strengths in the areas of education, experience, and skills. This is the time to pat yourself on the back and make a list of all those things you're so gosh darn good at. Maybe you're a captivating storyteller. Or maybe you've won every math competition known to mankind. Know your strengths and how to play them up in your résumé. If you say that you love art design, your classes, work experience, and accomplishments, such as awards won in art excellence, should attest to that. Be proud of what you've accomplished, and get ready to brag about it in your interview.

3. **Keep it easy to read.** Your résumé should be easy to understand in a 5- to 10- second scan. Use bullets to help your special qualities and essential work experience stand out clearly. Edit your text and cut superfluous statements and fillers so that only the essential remains. Agencies receive hundreds of applications each week, and human resources managers will toss long, rambling résumés without a second thought. Unless you've already had an extensive career, keep your résumé to one page.

4. **Organize your experience.** When putting your résumé together, you can organize your experience either chronologically or functionally. On a chronological résumé, list your education and employment in order, with the most recent experiences at the top. But if your educational background isn't so hot or your work experience is all over the map, a functional format, which lets you focus on specific abilities, may be the way to go. Organize a functional résumé around the following sections: Skills, Advertising Experience, Other Work Experience, and Education. If you went to an impressive school, by all means list your education at the top of your résumé; otherwise, list it at the bottom. Use the top part of each section for the qualities that employers are looking for in their entry-level employees: administrative skills, office experience, and computer skills. Be sure that your résumé is totally up-to-date. Revise it whenever you gain relevant experience (even if it's freelance), and try to account for any holes you may have.

5. **Use action words.** When describing your past experience, use action verbs such as *expanded, created, designed*, and *coordinated*. It's always better to start your bullet points with "Managed a 20-person team . . ." or "Controlled $2,000 in finances . . ." rather than "Had the opportunity to . . ." or "Spent a lot of time working with . . ." Present yourself with power and get right to the point.

6. **Make sure your résumé tells your story.** Your résumé should tell a clear, coherent story about who you are and what you bring to the table. If your main goal is to convince an agency that you are a people person, but everything on your résumé shouts "independence" and

"solitary work," an interviewer won't hear the story you want to tell her. Give your résumé to a few people and ask them what they think the key message is. If they don't give the answer you were hoping for, it's time for some revisions.

7. **Make it professional.** There's no room for sloppiness on your résumé. Employers are looking for easy ways to eliminate candidates, and spotting just one typo on a résumé will give them a reason to toss it. Eliminate all spelling errors and make sure everything looks clean and elegant. Align dates and headers and use a standard font (no flowery scripts!). Use a simple, modest email address that clearly incorporates your name. "Iamanadvertisinggod@wonderfulme.com" and "hotchick@gogirl.com" are not appropriate.

8. **Include interesting tidbits.** Don't get über-personal about your hair color, pants size, or musical tastes, but you can always add a little personality to your résumé. Even if the details you include don't relate directly to advertising, seeing that you were on the varsity fencing team in college or that you write reviews of country music in your spare time might interest potential employers. Keep these tidbits to a minimum, though, since you don't want to take valuable space away from more relevant items.

9. **Seek wise counsel.** If you have personal contacts in the business, ask them to take a look at your résumé. Investigate the resources at your campus career center. Meet with a career advisor, get a password to the college's online job board, and find out if your school has a reciprocity agreement with a marketing or media school or program that might share resources.

10. **Do a real-world check.** Find job listings for positions similar to the ones you're interested in, examine the requirements mentioned, and see how your résumé measures up. If you've got most of the requirements covered, you'll be seen as a competitive candidate. If you don't, figure out how you can tweak your experience (without lying!) to fill in the gaps.

If you didn't go to a school that offered an advertising or a marketing major, don't panic. Employers also look favorably on a liberal arts background that gives you a broad and well-rounded education.

The résumé-writing process can be a slow one, and you shouldn't rush through it. Be honest with yourself when outlining your interests, strengths, and weaknesses. Craft *your* story. Make sure your résumé is compelling, grammatically perfect, and complete with the most updated information. It might seem like a long, stressful road, but this is the next big step in your life we're talking about here. When you accept that perfect job offer in a few weeks or months, you'll thank yourself for taking the time to put together such a killer package.

SAMPLE RÉSUMÉS

In the next section, we'll show you the résumés of three aspiring advertising giants seeking entry-level jobs. Each applicant comes to the table with very different backgrounds, but they all follow the 10 steps to perfection, creating clear, well-designed résumés that broadcast their strengths loud and clear. Read their résumés and our commentaries, then get inspired to write your own!

SAMPLE RÉSUMÉ—CREATIVE

Kevin Cohen
9500 Mass Avenue
Boston, MA 55555
617-555-5555 (mobile)
31arts@email.com

Objective
Motivated self-starter seeks junior art director position at leading advertising agency.

Education
New York Design School   *New York, NY*
Fall 2001–Spring 2005
Majored in graphic design for websites, graduating with honors (3.6 GPA)
Managed re-design of the website for the school's summer internship program to make it more appealing and user-friendly

Qualifications
Common Technologies: XHTML, CSS, Flash, JavaScript, Apache, 3D Studio Max, Premiere & After Effects (video editing)
Macromedia: QuarkXPress, Fireworks, Flash, Dreamweaver
Adobe: Photoshop, Image Ready, Illustrator, Acrobat (PDF documents)

Experience
31 Arts Studio, Owner/Freelancer   *Boston, MA*
2004–Present
- Operate all business functions of privately owned web-design company
- Design and hand-code websites for private and professional clients, including companies and organizations (see portfolio for examples of unique work)
- Conceive and communicate layout, schedule, and design plan based on client needs
- Develop, including copyedit, deliverables in a timely fashion based on approved plan
- Follow entire life cycle of web site from search engine optimization and registration to implementing updates and site management

HyperGate Magazine   *Boston, MA*
2005–Present
- Contribute articles to monthly magazine on emerging trends in web design
- Write and illustrate sci-fi comic strip *The Perilous Accounts of Dexter X. McFlash*

BBDO—Graphic Design Intern   *San Francisco, CA*
Summer 2004
- Assisted art director with client marketing and branding projects
- Worked on new business pitch for youth-oriented energy drink
- Accompanied the art director on various internal and client meetings

Portfolio and References Available upon Request

What's So Great About Kevin's Résumé?

1. **The story is clear.** Kevin indicates the exact role he's looking for in his objective statement. Kevin lists his education front and center then launches into his qualifications as a clear indication of his credentials.

2. **The organization is logical.** He organizes his résumé in such a way as to highlight both his technical skills and his strong work ethic and business sense. For someone lacking extensive experience in advertising, he makes a strong case for why he deserves a look.

3. **Action words are used to emphasize strengths.** Though his recent work as an independent freelancer signals that he may not be used to office life, Kevin uses action words, such as *operate, design,* and *contribute* to clearly present his business savvy and strengths as a worker.

4. **Related work is indicated.** Kevin does have some practical experiences that relate to advertising—heavy client-oriented work as a freelancer and interning experience at an ad agency. He also includes his magazine work, which demonstrates that he keeps up with current trends and is creative beyond his work life.

5. **Portfolio and references are made available.** Prospective employers will want to see proof of Kevin's ability and range. He makes it clear that he is prepared to show this and back it up with recommendations.

SAMPLE RÉSUMÉ—ACCOUNT MANAGEMENT

Trisha Millrose
81 George Washington Street, Morris, NJ 09123
Phone: 555-555-5555; email: millrose@college.edu

OBJECTIVE: To secure entry-level position in Account Management.

EDUCATION
Tufts University (Fall 2002–Spring 2006)
Cambridge, MA; BA with honors, Psychology
GPA: 3.8
Study Abroad: Oxford, England

EXPERIENCE
Kaleidoscope Advertising Agency (Summer 2005)
   Intern, Account Management
- Researched the competitive landscape for telecom advertisements
- Assisted in presentations for company executives and client
- Managed production schedule for upcoming print ad campaigns
- Updated weekly status sheets for account management team
- Wrote creative briefs for upcoming television commercials

Facebook (Summer 2004)
   Intern, Marketing
- Created media kits for sales team
- Assisted in marketing efforts for Facebook Mobile Project
- Managed expenses and schedule for marketing team

Special Olympics (Summer 2003)
   Intern, Operations
- Managed planning and logistics for large summer fund-raiser
- Assisted with research & planning for yearly summer games
- Coordinated with local organizational leaders in establishing best practices

ACTIVITIES and AWARDS
Student Government (Fall 2005–Spring 2006)
   Tufts University, Vice President
- Chaired 30-member student government committee representing campus life
- Implemented and coordinated SpringFest and other major student life initiatives

Student Theatrical Society (Fall 2003 –Spring 2006)
   Tufts University, Business & Marketing Manager
- Managed marketing initiatives for largest student theatrical society on campus
- Increased revenue for theatrical society by 75% over three-year tenure

Varsity Tennis Team (Fall 2002–Spring 2006)
   Tufts University, Player and Publicity Manager
- Northeastern Championships in Fall 2005
- As Publicity Manager increased fan attendance by 30%

ADDITIONAL SKILLS/INTERESTS
- Proficient in written and spoken French
- Extensive experience with Microsoft Word, Microsoft Excel, PowerPoint, and Photoshop

What's So Great About Trisha's Résumé?

1. **Her presentation is crisp and appealing.** Trisha's résumé is pleasing to look at. Her headings are clear. Bold and italics indicate different information in a subtle way. All of the information she wants to communicate is there for the viewing.

2. **Bullets point to key skills.** Bullet points are easily scannable, and there's no better way for quickly highlighting skills and experience.

3. **Her skills are action oriented.** Trisha uses strong words to indicate what she's done and is capable of doing. She also gives some variety, using different verbs to describe her experience. Even though she's not had much work experience beyond internships, she uses words, such as *managed, implemented,* and *coordinated* to present herself as confident and able.

4. **She backs up her accomplishments.** She doesn't just say she did a good job; she proves it. A 30 percent increase in attendance at varsity tennis games tells potential employers that she can achieve real results.

5. **She gives a little extra.** Beyond education and work, Trisha lists the programs she's worked with and likely to encounter in a work setting. She also lists an interest in French and role on the tennis team. These intangibles show that she's well rounded and has goals beyond work.

SAMPLE RÉSUMÉ—MEDIA SERVICES

Rafael Delgado

21 Palm St, Apt. 2, San Francisco, CA 84865
555-565-2135
rafaeld@email.edu

SUMMARY

Strong work ethic; proven leadership skills; experience in concept creation and implementation for promotional purposes

EDUCATION

University of San Francisco   **(Fall 2002–Spring 2006)**
BA, Communication Studies, GPA: 3.1
Specialized courses taken: Intro to Psychology, Applied Statistics, The Economics of Marketing, Advertising Strategies, Advertising Presentation, Persuasion and Social Influence

Writing for the Real World   **(2006)**
"False Cognates: Misrepresentations of Latino Culture in Mainstream Television" published in annual multidisciplinary student essay anthology

Men's Soccer Team   **(2002–2004)**
Named to West Coast Conference Second Team All-Conference in 2003

EXPERIENCE

Latin American Student Organization (LASO)   **(2004–2006)**
University of San Francisco, Secretary
- Spearheaded *Hola, Los Amigos* welcome week promotion, including creation of flyers and webpage, to introduce incoming students to LASO activities
- Helped conceive, coordinate, and execute on-campus events to promote awareness of Latin American culture and heritage
- Established and maintained relationships between LASO and San Francisco–based companies and non-profit organizations to aid in sponsorship and support

San Francisco Magazine   **(Summer 2005)**
San Francisco, Editorial Intern
- Floated between research and editorial departments
- Checked copy and conducted online research for reporters

Tower Records   **(2000–2004)**
San Francisco, Assistant Floor Manager
- Oversaw daily activities and schedule of cashiers and clerks
- Provided input on buying decisions for sales promotion efforts in local magazines, newspapers, and radio
- Assisted in development and creation of in-store displays

SKILLS

Fluent in written and spoken Spanish
Experience in MS Office, FileMaker Pro, and basic website creation and HTML programming

What's So Great About Rafael's Résumé?

1. **He works with what he has.** As a recent graduate, Rafael has little direct experience in advertising or media services—just a magazine internship and a few years in retail. But he does have proven skills that can transfer to a position in advertising. His work with the Latin American Student Organization provides evidence of his leadership and networking capabilities. Through this affiliation and his work experience, he clearly demonstrates a familiarity with promotion and sales.

2. **He highlights relevant educational experience.** Though his work experience isn't strong, Rafael wisely points out coursework directly related to advertising, psychology, and math—important for work in media services. References from professors who taught these courses could go a long way to enhancing Rafael's credentials, provided his grades were good.

3. **He demonstrates that he's well-rounded.** Throughout his résumé, Rafael displays a dedication and interest that goes beyond simple coursework. His publication in the student anthology provides evidence of his writing skills. His service to LASO indicates an interest in community service and cultural awareness. His accomplishments in soccer speak to his discipline and drive. All of these achievements demonstrate those intangibles that every employer looks for.

4. **His résumé is well-organized.** Since he's a recent grad, Rafael puts his educational information at the top, highlighting his coursework and accomplishments. He follows this with a concise description of his experience, explaining those items that speak best to his transferable skill sets. And because "advertising" doesn't leap off the page, he makes good use of a summary to zero in on those qualities that make him a good fit.

ASSEMBLE YOUR PORTFOLIO

If you are seeking a creative position, a portfolio is crucial for demonstrating your artistic and technical skills. Your portfolio should include of a variety of high-quality pieces that represent the depth and breadth of your talent. Although samples of actual advertising work are best, your portfolio doesn't necessarily have to contain professional-quality pieces: School assignments and extracurricular and personal projects are all acceptable if they are polished and neat.

It's always best to present your portfolio in person at the interview. This will give you a great opportunity to answer questions and help your potential employer to associate a face with a name. However, many agencies will ask that you submit pieces from your portfolio along with your résumé before they meet with you, so that they can get an idea of your abilities beforehand.

Choosing Your Work

Employers look for work that is original, creative, and heartfelt. Try to keep your portfolio to 12 to 15 pieces. Choose the ones you are most proud of but that also showcase the range of your abilities. While many of your pieces will simply be examples of your artistic output, it's best to include at least a few that are actually ad campaigns of some sort. If you haven't worked on an ad campaign before, consider creating a few samples in Photoshop (or even using magazine cutouts) for fictitious companies or reworking an existing campaign—just make sure the campaign wasn't created by the agency you're applying to! Aim for two to three versions of an ad for each sample "campaign" and make sure to clearly label it as "spec ad." If you can do it in a creative and concise way, you might even consider displaying the process of how you got to your final idea. After all, your potential employer wants to see that you can take a creative brief and create a winning concept.

If you're a potential copywriter, include samples that show your flair with words. Brevity counts. Although you'll want to display the range of your writing ability, each piece should demonstrate your ability to convey a clear message in just a few words. Include at least one lengthy piece to show that you can sustain interest over a long period

Copywriters' portfolios should avoid puns, wordplays, and clichés at all costs.

of time. But even the prose on your long pieces should be lean, focused, and persuasive—qualities your potential employer will be seeking. For an added bit of spice, come up with catchy headlines to label the different pieces in your portfolio. And please, don't forget to check your grammar and spelling!

10 Last-Minute Portfolio Additions

If you're thinking of applying for a creative position and your portfolio is, well, sparse, here are 10 last-minute ideas for building up your book:

1. Volunteer to create a fund-raising ad campaign for a nonprofit organization.

2. Create promotional materials for yourself as a freelancer— business cards and brochures with a personalized logo.

3. Design a website for yourself or someone else.

4. Offer your services for free to a startup or local small business.

5. Design posters or flyers for an upcoming school or community event.

6. Do creative work for a local community organization, religious group, or musical act—anything!

7. If you're a writer, start a blog or submit articles for online publication.

8. Help out designing materials for a political campaign—a local politician or even a student government race.

9. Design something for a friend's or family member's business.

10. Redo an existing ad campaign that you feel could use a refresher.

Staying On Target

Make your portfolio as relevant as possible to the individual agencies you're interviewing with. Don't be afraid to change things and swap some pieces in and out, depending on the situation. If you're interviewing for an agency that specializes in interactive advertising, a portfolio full of nothing but print ads won't get you very far. Likewise, if you're speaking with a creative director who works mostly on direct-mail pieces, weigh your portfolio more heavily with brochures.

Part of staying on target also involves changing and updating your portfolio often to reflect changing trends and patterns. As you learn a new graphics program or platform, include an example or your work in your portfolio. You want to show employers that you're not only creative but also fresh and cutting edge.

With online consumerism and media fragmentation, advertising in general is moving into an era where consumers are more in control of what they view and when. No matter what kind of agency you're applying to, creative directors are looking for people who can create in multiple mediums. Your portfolio should display variety in how you approach a single subject and an ability to adapt one message to many platforms.

66 I probably didn't appreciate the freedom I had as a prospective copywriter: no client and no committee to pass judgment. Portfolios are your opportunity to really let it rip. Don't hold back. Once you have a job, you'll never have that freedom again. Once clients are spending money, conservatism creeps in. Don't hold back in your portfolio."

—**Ty Montague,** Chief Creative Officer,
JWT

Presenting your Portfolio

As you're building your portfolio, keep your aesthetic wits about you. A boring manila folder or, worse, a bag full of chaotically assembled bits of paper won't fly. Splurge a little and print all your pieces on some high-quality paper—it's reasonably priced these days—and slip them into one of those nifty sleek black portfolio cases that you can find for about $20 at any office supply store. If you've made some direct-mail pieces, include originals if possible or use high-quality photographs of the pieces.

When organizing your portfolio, it's a good idea to create divider sections that group different categories of work together. This will help your future employer find what he's looking for quickly and easily. And just because they're divider pages doesn't mean they have to be boring. Use them to kill two birds with one stone: Show your peerless organizational abilities and your omnivorous creative drive. Create collages with bold headlines specific to each section. You're interviewing for a creative position, so get creative!

With more and more ad dollars shifting to online ventures, think about posting your portfolio on a website—preferably your own—or at least burning a digital version to a CD. You should always bring a print backup to interviews, but you'll find that it is becoming increasingly important to emphasize your technological prowess, and a nicely done digital portfolio accomplishes that quite subtly. Not to mention the time and postage you'll save directing people to your website rather than shipping samples all the time!

4

BECOMING AN EXPERT

Advertising is as much about *what* you know as *who* you know. The more informed you are, the more appealing you'll be to employers. So read up, get online, network, and explore your educational opportunities. Nothing beats a candidate who walks through the door brimming with confidence and the know-how to back it up. Here are some ways to really boost your ad IQ.

READ, READ, READ

Become a voracious, analytical consumer of media. Dog-ear magazine ads of special note. TiVo shows just to watch the commercials. Wander through your city's downtown area and look at the flashy billboards. As you consume your favorite media, pay special attention not only to the ads themselves, but also to how they are reaching you. A fully loaded campaign will include spots in magazines, newspapers, television, radio, and the Internet, along with a slick word-on-the-street component. Keep an eye on which brands are coming out with new major campaigns and what new tactics they are taking to get the message to the consumer.

But to really gain an in-depth understanding of where the industry is going and the minds that are behind the wheel, head to your local bookstore, library, or laptop and check out magazines, books, and websites on the advertising world. The following resources should make you well rounded enough to "speak advertising" with just about anybody, shy of David Ogilvy, perhaps . . .

Trade Magazines

These industry publications will keep you up-to-date on the latest news and help you scope out potential job opportunities. The magazines listed below tend to cover mainstream advertising and marketing topics, so if

Trade magazines are publications intended for readers working in specialized professions, as opposed to **consumer magazines** intended for the general public.

you're interested in more niche titles, a quick online search should point you in the right direction.

66 I think of *Us* and *PREMIERE* as trade publications. Since I have to keep current with hot celebrities, movies, trends, and culture, they can be handy tools. For instance, it's important not to cast a character you want to believe is a genuine 'husband' in a spot if you've just seen him in *US* magazine with his real wife. Plus, they're fun to read."

—**Jill Rothman,** Director of Production
JWT

- **Adweek,** adweek.com
  This weekly magazine covers all the fresh news in the advertising industry. This is *the* place to go for detailed info on accounts in review, client-agency relationships, movements among industry executives, and the hottest campaigns and award shows.

- **Advertising Age,** adage.com
  Another staple weekly news source, *Advertising Age* covers breaking industry news, the latest campaigns, people and players, new media, and account action.

- **BtoB Magazine,** btobonline.com
  The ultimate source for info on **business-to-business** marketing. Published monthly by Crain Communications, which also owns *Advertising Age*, *BtoB* includes articles and detailed information on marketing strategy.

- **Creativity,** adcritic.com
  Another one from Crain Communications, *Creativity* is a monthly magazine that can be a great resource for creatives and anyone else interested in the creative side of advertising. Along with the latest news and profiles of people in the field, there are informative articles on the cultural landscape of the advertising world. *Creativity*'s online

Business-to-business marketing refers to partnerships and transactions between two or more businesses, as opposed to business-to-consumer marketing, which directly targets the end consumer.

arm, adcritic.com, contains the additional content beyond what you'll find in the printed magazine.

For more resources: Visit the University of Washington's Foster Business Library at lib.washington.edu/business/guides/ad.html.

- ***Journal of Advertising,*** www.bus.iastate.edu/joa
  Combining theory with practical application, the *Journal of Advertising* examines advertising from philosophical, ethical, and sociological angles.

Recommended Books

There are tons of terrific books that can help you find everything from agency listings and current salary projections to life lessons on how to make it in the business from those who've done it. Here are just some of the must-reads you'll find in most libraries and bookstores.

- ***Standard Directory of Advertisers ("The Red Book"),*** National Register Publishing, annual publication
  This annual publication is basically the bible of advertising. Known industry-wide as "The Red Book," it is by far the most comprehensive printed source of information on thousands of ad agencies in the United States, covering the agencies, clients, and top executives on each major account.

- ***The Advertising Age Encyclopedia of Advertising,*** Routledge, 2002
  This three-volume resource includes detailed profiles of over 100 ad agencies around the world, essays on the industry, biographies of major players and profiles of significant Fortune 500 advertisers, and information on leading brands and campaigns.

- ***Ogilvy on Advertising,*** by David Ogilvy, Crown, 1983
  When one of the biggest names in advertising writes a book on the industry, it's probably a good idea to read it. Widely considered to be an essential read for anyone looking to break in, this book is an informative and inspirational look at the business.

- ***The Book of Gossage,*** by Howard Luck Gossage, The Copy Workshop, 1995
  Although not as well known a name as Ogilvy, Gossage was a pioneer in the '50s and '60s and is considered by many to have changed the face of

advertising through his consumer-driven approach. Essays written by Gossage, "The Socrates of San Francisco," as he was known, and others whom he's influenced reveal the man and his philosophy.

- ***A Century of American Icons,*** by Mary Cross, Greenwood Publishing Group
With an eye toward the industry's effect on popular culture, *A Century of American Icons* details the ad campaigns and slogans that defined twentieth-century consumerism. A great survey text, it organizes products and ad campaigns by decade and includes essays on the most influential ones.

Logging On

The Internet is a great place to do detailed research. Sign up for weekly newsletters or updates from online trade newspapers and visit advertising industry blogs on a regular basis. And if you're cramming for that interview tomorrow, you can always turn to Google for some last-minute research. Check out these websites to make sure you're up-to-date on your industry news.

- **Advertising Age,** adage.com
The online counterpart to the printed periodical, adage.com is a great place to look up data and timelines about the industry, as well as see lists of the best campaigns, ads, and jingles.

- ***Creativity's AdCritic,*** adcritic.com
The online face of *Creativity* magazine, this website is a great tool for prospective creatives, with current news, opinions, and critiques on the latest campaigns. Much of the goodies on this site come with a paid subscription only, but insiders will tell you it's well worth it.

- **VNU eMedia,** vnuemedia.com
A great reference site with links to daily advertising and marketing newsletters, media magazines and news sources, and general retail and service industry sites. This is the perfect one-stop shop for all things consumer.

- **American Association of Advertising Agencies,** www.aaaa.org
  The AAAA is the national trade association representing advertising agencies. Their website contains tons of information about the ad industry, including conference and seminar announcements, agency information, and a who's who. It also offers SmartBrief, a free daily email newsletter that covers the top ad industry news stories.

- **American Advertising Federation,** www.aaf.org
  The American Advertising Federation, the oldest trade association for advertising, hosts this site. Headquartered in D.C., AAF represents thousands of professionals in the advertising industry. Its website has news, info, and lots of resources intended specifically for college students.

- **Hoover's,** hoovers.com
  Hoover's is a terrific resource for information on thousands of publicly and privately held companies around the world. It includes links to company websites, annual financial reports, and main competitors. Be warned, however, that gaining access to the best information requires an expensive paid subscription to the Hoover's service.

Don't believe everything you Google!

The quality and accuracy of the information available online varies drastically from site to site. Evaluate what you read carefully. Keep the following points in mind before you fire up that browser.

Sponsored links: When you use a search engine such as Ask or Google, be wary of which links you decide to click on. Some of the most prominently placed links are "sponsored" links, which means that the company paid for that prime Internet real estate. Don't assume that they're necessarily the most reliable.

Company bias: Some websites have a clear point of view—often because they're shilling for a company pushing a product. Be wary. If a website seems to be selling you something, chances are, it is.

Impartiality: When researching schools or programs online, make sure your information comes from a truly independent source. Some seemingly impartial sites are actually subsidized by schools, and so the information you'll get from them will be skewed and possibly inaccurate.

READ BETWEEN THE BLOGS

Blogs written by people who work in the industry are a great way to get an unfiltered take on what life is like for advertising employees. Here are three of the best.

- **Adrants,** adrants.com
  Written by advertising vet Steve Hall, this blog is full of witty commentary on the advertising industry. Be warned: Many of the items are anything but G-rated. As MarketingSherpa.com said upon naming Adrants Best Advertising Blog of the year, "Sex sells."

- **Seth Godin's Blog,** sethgodin.typepad.com
  A very popular marketing blog written by industry author Seth Godin. Read his commentary on everything remotely related to marketing, from the interview process to human nature itself.

- **5 Blogs Before Lunch,** daveibsen.typepad.com/5_blogs_before_lunch/
  Created by consumer and technology marketing consultant David Allen Ibsen, this award-winning blog covers all the news and opinions on marketing, advertising, and branding.

NETWORK

Gossip is not always an indulgence, and when you're doing your initial job search, it can be a lifesaver. Warm up those vocal cords and talk to everyone you know. That golf buddy of your dad's might just know the art director at Wieden+Kennedy. And that quirky guy you met at a party and added to your MySpace friends list may know the new assistant account exec at McCann Erickson.

Make a list of everyone you know directly and everyone you know within one or two degrees of separation. When you've exhausted your list of personal acquaintances, talk to *their* personal acquaintances. Leave no stone unturned. Someone is bound to know somebody who can help you, give you contacts in the advertising industry, or at least provide you with valuable insight into the job search process.

Be super-organized about your contacts. Even if you're blessed with a photographic memory, you won't remember every bit of advice from everyone unless you write it all down. Keep detailed notes on whom you talk to, what they say, who they put you in touch with, and what steps you'll take next. There's no worse way to start a professional relationship than by forgetting how you know the creative director who has just granted you an informational interview.

Got organization?

Set up an Excel spreadsheet, Word document, or Access database to keep track of your networking efforts. If you prefer the glory of handwriting, devote a notebook or address book solely to this endeavor. List all your contacts and how you know them. Note their position and place of work. Keep track of the date and content of each interaction you have. Take notes as you're talking to them, and after the conversation is over, jot down follow-up thoughts. Think of this database as your personal networking bible!

Contacting Professionals

Keep your eyes open for the following networking opportunities.

- **Conversation:** Every day presents dozens of opportunities to network. Whether you're on the bus, in a class, or at a party, everyone you meet is a potentially useful contact. Networking often occurs spontaneously, but you can take active steps to make it happen. Go to informational forums, discussions, and lectures. Introduce yourself to the speaker afterward and talk to other interested members of the audience. You never know who you'll meet.

- **Phone:** Although it might seem old-fashioned, the phone is still a great way to follow up with someone you've recently met. Voice-to-voice interaction can make more of an impression than a simple email because it suggests that you care enough to put forth an extra effort. But calling someone you don't know well can be scary. Start by reminding the contact of where you met or explaining how you got their name ("Hi, Ms. Jones. You don't know me, but I saw your name in the alumni directory . . ."). Most of the time, people will be happy to speak with you.

- **Email:** Phones are more personal, but email is the easiest and quickest way to network, particularly when dealing with someone in a senior position. Bear in mind that professionals are bombarded with emails on a daily basis, so keep your message succinct. To avoid being relegated to the spam folder, use a descriptive, professional subject line ("SVA senior from last night's event"). In your message, mention how you know the person and be clear about why you are writing. As for tone, it's okay to make a joke or two or refer to moments from an earlier conversation, but if you're writing with the intention of eventually getting a job, keep your note fairly formal. If your email address is something like "hotchick97@email.com", create a new email address that includes your first and last name. Don't be alarmed if it takes a few days to get a response, but be sure that your follow-up is prompt.

66 I got into advertising by mistake. I had dropped out of college, was bored, and moved to New York. I got a job bartending and met someone who said, 'Hey, you'd be good at advertising.' "

—**Ty Montague,** Chief Creative Officer
JWT

- **Affiliations:** When you're part of a large organization, knowing 10 people is really more like knowing 50. Make a list of every organization you are or have been part of. That one month you spent in the Girl Scouts in sixth grade might not be very useful, but you'll get a lot of mileage out of that semester spent volunteering for Habitat for Humanity or the church you attended for 10 years. Religious groups, sports teams, charities or nonprofit organizations, internships, music or theater groups, and fraternities or sororities are all terrific

The American Advertising Federation (AAF) holds regular meetings with guest speakers and is open to students. The AAF also holds an annual student advertising competition.

for networking. Contact fellow members. Don't be shy about letting them know that you're looking for a job in advertising and never underestimate the importance of the coffee date. People are apt to help out those who are members of their group. And chances are good that someday you'll have the opportunity to return the favor.

COLLECTING BUSINESS CARDS

Don't hesitate to ask for business cards whenever you go to an industry event, lecture, or reception; most people love to hand them out. Within a few days of getting a business card, follow up with an email or phone call. Leave a short, straightforward message that serves as a friendly reminder that you exist and are hunting for a job.

Networking for the Week

Advertising Week is an annual international industry event organized in the fall at locations throughout New York City. It includes speeches, panels, presentations, public exhibits, expositions, galas, and entertainment—Gnarls Barkley performed in 2006. First held in 2004, Advertising Week was conceived by the AAAA with the expressed goal of celebrating creativity in the industry and "inspiring young people to join the craft." It is the single biggest industry event, and everyone who is anyone in the field attends. So should you. For more info, go to advertisingweek.com.

With all the networking opportunities you are actively pursuing, you should be gathering quite a stack of cards! As your collection grows, it's important to keep track of the date and event where you gathered each one. These cards might be the ticket to your future job, so keep them well organized and easily accessible.

Following Up—Without Stalking

Advertising professionals are very busy, and you won't always get the warm, speedy reply that you desire. Be patient and polite and give people a few days to respond to you. Once that window of optimal response time passes, remind your contact of your conversation without coming across as a pest. There is a fine line between polite encouragement and offensive badgering. Here are a few ways to stay on the right side of the line.

1. **Include action items in your message.** Simple "Nice to meet you" notes often fail to elicit a response on their own. To stop your contact from taking a glance, smiling, then forgetting all about it, outline some reasonable next steps that she can respond to easily. For example, you might suggest setting up an informational interview or asking for the contact info of someone they mentioned you should get in touch with.

2. **Allow response time.** If you've suggested a next step and don't hear back within a week or two, you can follow up with an email or a phone call to reiterate your request. If you receive an out-of-office auto response, give the person an extra few weeks before writing again. You want to come across as a go-getter without seeming aggressive.

Follow-up etiquette

What you're thinking:

"Remember me? I know you're busy, and I bet I got buried in your in-box. Well, here I am again! I won't let you forget about me *that* easily!"

What you actually say:

"Hi! It was great meeting you last Monday. I'm just following up on my previous email in regard to setting up an informational interview. I'm really excited to hear about your experiences in the industry. Please let me know if there is a time next week that will work for you. Thanks!"

3. **Send updates.** A good way to preserve a professional contact without pestering is to send a note every so often with updates on your recent progress. If you have completed an advertising internship or received high honors in related coursework, it is definitely appropriate to keep your contact informed.

Informational Interviews

Informational interviews, as the name suggests, are informal meetings held for the purpose of gathering information rather than filling a job opening. They are opportunities for you to learn about a professional's job, the company she works for, and the industry in general. They can be conducted over the phone or in person, at the offices of your contact, or over coffee or lunch in the neighborhood.

Informational interviews can help you pinpoint the area of advertising that is right for you or provide more depth in an area you know you want to get into. You'll have the chance to ask for advice on your résumé and on the best way to approach your job search. Everyone you will talk to was a newbie once and should have some valuable career advice to impart.

Informational interviews are also a great way to make contacts at an agency that isn't hiring at the time but might be soon. Although you are there to listen and learn, you should take any appropriate opportunity to talk about your own experiences and plans.

Securing an informational interview is an extension of successful networking. Contact people who share affiliations with you, get in touch with family friends and friends of friends, and attend industry events and career fairs. Reach out to these potential informational interviewers with a phone call or personalized email (no mass emails, please!). Write with a specific action item: "I am interested in setting up an informational interview to learn more about your experiences in the industry. Do you have any free time during the week of November 2?" You'll be pleasantly surprised by how many people are willing to help.

> Don't try to turn an informational interview into a job interview! People generally get annoyed if they offer you their expertise and realize that all you want is a job.

PREPARING FOR THE INTERVIEW

Prepare for your informational interview by taking the following few steps.

- **Get informed.** Read up on the company and the individual you'll be meeting with. Visit the company website. Use your resources to find recent news articles about your contact's work and any new products, accounts, mergers, and deals she or the company has been involved in. Come up with a few discussion items to show that you are well versed in current business events and are familiar with the company. If you appear knowledgeable and informed, you are more likely to spark a more in-depth conversation and make a stellar first impression.

- **Look professional.** Even though you're not going after a specific job, you want to make the best impression possible. If you show up on time, dress in business attire, conduct yourself in a polite and pleasant manner, and behave professionally, it'll be easier for your contact to envision you fitting in at his agency. These interviews are a great networking resource, and you want the interviewer to feel that he can recommend you to others.

- **Come with questions.** Informational interviews are usually set up by you, as opposed to the interviewer. That means that you bear the responsibility for setting the agenda. The following questions are always safe starters:

  > *How did you find yourself in the advertising industry?*
  > *What do you enjoy most about working in advertising?*
  > *What has your career path looked like?*
  > *What advice do you have for someone first entering the advertising industry?*

  And if you've done your research, you should be able to ask intelligent follow-up questions, while also inserting some clever tidbits about yourself.

It's okay to take a few notes during an informational interview, but you want to appear engaged. Don't write down every word. Focus on making eye contact, remembering the key points, and jotting down just a few notes now and then. Immediately after the interview, write down a more detailed account.

FOLLOWING UP

If someone takes the time to give you an informational interview, you should take the time to thank her. It's only fair. Emails are fine, though a handwritten card might make more of an impression. And don't stop at the thank-you. Reiterate your enthusiasm for the industry after talking with her. Mention something she said that had a particularly profound effect on you. If she gave you another contact name, indicate your intention to get in touch with that person (and don't waste time getting in touch with him!).

CONSIDER FURTHER EDUCATION

To compete for some positions, you have to make the personal investment in further education. We know, we know: You thought you left school far behind when you tossed your cap into the air. But sometimes a little continuing education can go a long way, especially if the job you're gunning for requires specialized skills such a graphic design, computer programming, or production expertise.

Classes are a huge commitment of energy (not to mention money), and before jumping in, you'll want to decide if this is really the right move for you. Don't go back to school just to go. Many advertising positions do not require a specialized degree in marketing or advertising. In fact, many agencies prefer a liberal arts background. On-the-job training or an internship or two may suffice. However, if you have thoroughly assessed the situation and you feel that the added knowledge, experience, and industry connections will benefit you, school may be the answer.

If you want a creative position but don't have a strong portfolio there are lots of short-term programs out there specifically designed to help you create one.

Good Reasons to Go Back

You certainly don't need a specialized degree to make it in advertising. But if any of these descriptions ring true, you might want to peruse the courses being offered at universities in your area.

- Many people in the position you want have an advanced degree or have taken courses in a specific area.

- In your chosen path, an advanced degree will give you more credibility.

- The skill set or specialized knowledge that school will provide will be more useful than on-the-job training or internships.

66 The best courses are at the art or advertising schools, taught by people in the industry with the goal of helping students create their books. It fills the gap between not being able to get a job without a book and not being able to put a book together without a job."

—Jill Rothman, Director of Production
JWT

Good Reasons *Not* to Go Back

On the other hand, if you fit the descriptions below you may want to exercise some caution before piling on the debt. You can learn a lot—for free and on your own time—from the library and the Internet, so make sure you've exhausted all your options before jumping back on the school wagon.

- You're not sure you'll be in advertising five years from now.

- You think advertising sounds cool and sexy, but you haven't had any experience yet. An internship would be a better (and cheaper) way to test the waters and see how you like the industry.

- You already hold a degree in advertising or another relevant area, and those extra courses wouldn't make much difference on your résumé. You're better off applying for an entry-level job or training program aimed at applicants with your current skill set and education level.

- You're not sure you could handle the commitment of time and money at this stage. Figure out how much you'll need to save to take classes further down the road, and work out a budget.

Tuition Help

Some other notable advertising programs:

The Creative Circus (creativecircus.com)

Art Center College of Design (artcenter.edu)

Miami Ad School (miamiadschool.com)

School of Visual Arts (schoolofvisualarts.edu)

Going back to school can be particularly daunting if you're still paying off loans on another degree. Here are a few tips on funding further education.

- **Start with your public library.** Research scholarships and grants offered by local businesses, larger corporations, and philanthropic organizations.

- **Call the schools you're applying to or look online.** Find out if there are scholarships available. A surprising number of funding opportunities go untapped because nobody applies for them!

- **Look into federal work-study opportunities and on-campus employment.** Full-time university employees often get free tuition as part of their benefits package, meaning you can work by day and learn by night.

- **Check out jobs that offer tuition assistance.** You might be able to pay for school and further your search for the perfect advertising job at the same time.

66 The best college for advertising is life—understanding people and their motivations."

—**Ty Montague,** Chief Creative Officer
JWT

Evaluating Schools

You obviously want to work in advertising, but what are you really looking to get out of your education? To start, you'll want to know if a chosen school does the following:

- Teaches the **material** you need to learn.

- Employs **faculty** with current experience and connections in their field.

- Offers the **degree** you need to get the job you want.

- Offers **job placement,** has strong **alumni connections,** and offers useful **career services.**

- Is **affordable** or offers the financial aid you need to avoid feeling overburdened.

- Is **flexible** and accommodates you whether you are a full-time or part-time student.

- Supports for-credit **internships** at major companies or helps you get substantial summer jobs in the industry (upon request, they should provide you with a list of internships its students have held in the past two years).

5

INTERNING

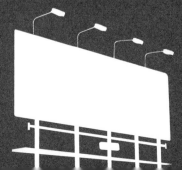

Welcome to the next link in the career food chain: the internship. Your brief gig as an unpaid (usually) working stiff will probably not offer you in-depth involvement in meaningful projects. But you will get a real feel for how the industry works, how people spend their time, and what the culture is like. You'll be introduced to the skill sets necessary to compete in the market, and you'll get a prime opportunity to secure the contacts you'll need when your job search gets under way. Plus you'll get to see whether advertising is really the career for you. In this chapter, we'll take you through the process of landing a solid internship and then making the most of it.

DEFINE THE INTERNSHIP

Internships allow students and recent graduates to learn how to apply their education to a job by assisting and observing in a professional environment. They usually require a minimum three-month commitment and are unpaid or offer a low hourly wage or stipend.

Many large companies have highly structured intern programs that include weekly meetings, official company mentors, introductions to high-level company execs, and field trips. If you are accepted to one of these programs, you will likely be part of a class of interns, in which you may forge some strong relationships. An internship at a smaller agency may be less structured (you might be the only intern), but you'll likely take on more responsibility and get experience in a variety of areas, from strategy planning to design creation for smaller campaigns. If you can get in touch with people who have interned at the company before, ask what their experiences were like.

The "Unpaid Slave"

Employers often complain that interns feel above menial tasks such as filing, photocopying, and note taking. Although they want their interns to have a positive and meaningful experience, interns are temporary employees and exist on the lowest rung of the career ladder, meaning their work is often of the basic administrative nature. You won't be running a department, and it's unlikely that the work you do will change the advertising landscape as we know it.

Some interns will tell you that their official title should be "Unpaid Slave." But here's the real deal: Experience always pays off! You might be doing nothing more than making zillions of copies. But you're still taking in everything around you and learning from everyone you work with, even if you don't realize it at the time. Your employers will be judging your attitude just as much as (or even more than) your skill level. And understanding what it's like to be at the bottom of the food chain will help you relate to people for the rest of your career.

No matter what the setting, it's important to go into your first internship with realistic expectations, plenty of patience, and a lot of enthusiasm. A good attitude and a hard work ethic will go a long, long way. Here are some of the situations and responsibilities you can expect as an intern.

66 One day I was watching a commercial shoot, the next day I was researching current trends in the hair care products market. I got to work with performers from the documentary *Rize,* which was pretty amazing. I spent an afternoon wandering through Toys "R" Us with my supervisor to gain insights into the world of kids today. From brainstorming meetings to client conference calls, interns get to see a lot. And the people in advertising are fun and unpredictable. On my first day, I was shot in the back with a Nerf gun by one of my bosses!"

—**Brianne Janacek,** Intern
Saatchi & Saatchi

INTERN IN ACCOUNT MANAGEMENT

Interns in account management departments handle a wide variety of tasks. On any given day, you might be handling basic administrative work, conducting research for a particular project, accompanying team members to meetings with the creative teams and clients, or helping to organize team events and status meetings.

Account management interns handle a lot of administrative work. You'll be assisting with scheduling, researching, proofing, organizing, and note taking. Agencies look for people who are organized and hardworking. General social skills and professional behavior are very important, as are leadership qualities and a team player attitude. You won't be winning clients or participating in high-power decision making, but you will be assisting those who are, and you'll have the chance to soak up a lot of wisdom in the process.

Tasks and Responsibilities

Here are some tasks you can expect to perform as an account management intern.

- **Competitive research:** Good advertisers know what the competition is up to. Interns collect print, TV, and direct-mail or online ads produced by competitive brands and may be asked to provide a summary for the rest of the team and updates when necessary.

- **Scheduling:** Ad campaigns have many moving parts, and to finish a campaign on time, every stage (creation, approvals, revisions) must adhere to a hard-and-fast deadline. The intern may keep track of these deadlines for the team.

- **Portfolio management:** Most teams keep a team portfolio—a detailed record of all the work they've done and the projects they've completed. This is especially important if the team works on lots of direct-mail and online ads, which come out at high frequency. The intern may be responsible for keeping the team's portfolio organized and up-to-date.

- **Getting materials to clients:** Does the client need a copy of the latest revisions to their commercial spot or color samples of magazine ads for a meeting with company executives? Getting the duplicates made and hand-delivering them or messengering them over to the client often falls to the intern.

SAMPLE INTERNSHIP LISTING

Account Management Intern for growing
Interactive Advertising Agency in Dallas, TX

A growing interactive agency currently has an opening for an Account Management intern. The candidate chosen will gain hands-on experience working in a rapidly growing agency and will work directly with an Account Executive on important client relationships. We will provide this hardworking, dedicated candidate with the opportunity to perform in, and experience, the work environment in an advertising agency.

The program runs from June 15 through August 15. The intern will receive minimum wage during the summer and will be given a $1,000 stipend for college tuition and expenses at the close of the program.

Applicants for this position must fill out an application form and submit it no later than March 31. The following criteria must be met by all applicants:

- Be a full-time student with a minimum cumulative 3.00 GPA (or the equivalent).

- Have attained at least junior standing at the start of internship.

- Be returning to your college for the fall term after the internship.

- Provide a letter of recommendation from one professor with whom you have taken a course in the current academic year.

Interviews will be conducted in April, and final decisions will be made in early May.

- **Assisting on photo and video shoots:** Photo and video shoots are always a ton of work. While the creative team determines the vision of the shoot, the client oversees and the account management team helps out. Interns are expected to run small errands, keep the client happy, and lend a hand in any way necessary, which likely means getting drinks or delivering messages.

- **Proofreading:** If one word of an ad is misspelled or if one punctuation mark is wrong, it's a total disaster. You may be asked to lend an extra pair of eyes.

- **Note taking:** Account management departments meet often with the client, with the creatives, and with everyone else. Interns may be asked to play scribe at these meetings.

- **Assisting at events:** If an agency is holding an event, such as a campaign launch or a client party, interns will most likely be asked to pitch in and lend a hand. This will mostly involve setting up, greeting and handing out name badges, passing out promotional material or gifts, and running last-minute errands. You may even get to enjoy yourself once your work is over!

- **Managing the status reports:** If your team is busy with lots of projects, you may be in charge of a status report that keeps everyone informed about schedule and status. Duties would entail taking notes at team meetings, updating the report, and answering questions on particular projects.

❝ During my internship, I worked directly for two account managers and one account executive. They were my unofficial mentors. It was very helpful working with them, and they were always open to giving me tips and answering questions. Also, my client was Coors, and I got to attend the VIP party and concert for the Coors Light Mountain Jam. So much fun!"

—**Brooke Firchow,** Assistant Account Executive
DDB

INTERN IN CREATIVE

Creative interns get to assist some of the most imaginative brains in the business—or at least say hi to them a couple of times. Because there's a higher premium placed on previous experience compared with other account management or media, interning is a terrific (some would even say vital) way to start out for a prospective creative. Making contacts, building your portfolio, and getting your feet wet on a couple of real projects will improve your chances of landing a paid freelance position or full-time junior copywriter or art director role.

Agencies hiring creative interns usually look for students with specific skills in graphic design, copywriting, or studio arts. You might start out by assisting a copywriter or art director with some projects and build your way up from there. Or you might be asked to help with a new business pitch or a pro bono assignment. Agencies always have multiple projects in the works, and as an intern with writing or design skills, you may find yourself doing more than just pushing papers.

> **Giving back while getting in**
>
> Many large ad agencies will take on pro bono accounts for local or national nonprofits. In some cases, the agency will hire an official team to work on the ad campaign and will pay them regular salaries even though the campaign does not bring in any incremental revenue. But often agencies will use these pro bono projects for training programs and internships, where green employees form task teams to come up with creative ad campaigns and fund-raising solutions. Pro bono assignments at Ogilvy & Mather have included the New York Public Library and the New York chapter of the Special Olympics. Clients are typically organizations where the agency CEO or another senior executive sits on the board, or they may be part of a new business pitch for the agency.

Tasks and Responsibilities

Here are some tasks you can expect to perform as a creative intern.

- **Creating boards:** New creative concepts are presented to everyone from the creative director to the account team and client. As the intern, it will be your job to mount the concepts on presentation boards so that they look professional and organize them in a visually appealing, easy-to-follow way.

Warning: You are not the head of the creative team!

You have lots of brilliant ideas for campaigns. You see ads on TV and know you could do much better. Keep it to yourself. It's okay to present your ideas if you're asked to help with the creative brainstorming process, but be careful to not overstep your boundaries by critiquing someone's work too vigorously or going over your supervisor's head to present an idea to the art director. The creatives have worked hard to get where they are, and they know more than you do. Don't keep good ideas to yourself—you want to win recognition—but be professional and respectful and follow the proper chain of command if you want to suggest something.

- **Assisting on photo and video shoots:** Photo and video shoots involve many tasks, from choosing the location to picking talent and gathering props. You may be onsite to do last-minute errands and adjustments and help out the art director as needed.

66 Earlier this week, I got to go to my first photo shoot. It was on location at a winery. I helped with the props, and my supervisor even let me look in the viewfinder of the camera and asked me my opinion on the shots. I felt like a full-blown art director!"

—**Brittany Fleitman,** Intern
Fogarty Klein Monroe

- **Scheduling:** Most creative teams work on many campaigns at the same time, all with multiple (and sometimes conflicting) deadlines. It may be your role as intern to manage these schedules, sort out conflicts, and help remind the team of pending deadlines.

- **Managing portfolios:** Creative teams also keep samples of all the work they have produced for their clients. As an intern, you may be responsible for keeping those samples organized and labeled, updating them, and ordering more if need be.

INTERN IN MEDIA SERVICES

Like account management, internships in this area are a good place to get a broad perspective on the entire advertising industry. Although the trend for the past couple of decades has been to move media services away from account management and creative, this has been changing in recent years. As interactive media finds synergies with more traditional forms of advertising, media planning is finding itself drawn closer and closer to the complete campaign process, from the first client meetings to the actual campaign launch. Interns in media departments do everything from the usual administrative tasks, to research on particular products and companies, to sitting in on meetings with other departments and clients, to planning focus groups with consumers.

Similar to internships in account management, agencies hiring media interns look for people possessing strong organizational and communication skills. Though completion of specific coursework isn't always required, because media services tends to look for specialized degrees or specific classes taken when hiring full-time employees, interns may need to demonstrate that they're on this path.

Tasks and Responsibilities

Here are some tasks you can expect to perform as a media intern.

- **Researching:** People in media services analyze how members of the target market behave—what shows they watch, what they do online, and what radio stations they listen to. Interns generally assist planners and buyers with research that will help determine the best places to run their client's ads.

- **Scheduling:** Most ad campaigns run in several different places. A television commercial runs on many channels; an online ad runs on many websites. As an intern, you may help manage a detailed schedule of where the ads are running and confirm that they did in fact run as planned.

- **Attending meetings:** Many media companies will be vying for the client's dollars. Media buyers attend meetings where these companies try to persuade them that their website, magazine, or show is the best place to run the client's ads. You may be present at some of these meetings and may even get to toss in your two cents!

- **Sending materials to clients:** If the client wants a copy of the commercial they are running on the Discovery Channel or an issue of *Forbes* magazine with their ad on the inside cover, it may be your responsibility to get these materials to them at lightning speed.

- **Note taking:** There are meetings, meetings, and meetings . . . with account execs, art directors, and others in the agency. You may be asked to sit in and take notes that the team can use for reference later on.

- **Attending events:** Going to events, being wined and dined . . . it's all part of working in a media department. As an intern, you'll hopefully get to attend at least a few of these functions. It's bad form for an agency not to be represented at an event for one of their clients. If other people can't make it, it's not out of the realm of possibility that you may be asked to accompany an account exec. So brush up on your dinner conversation.

- **Managing status reports:** You guessed it: Status reports are generally a ubiquitous fixture of all internships. Like an account management intern, you may be asked to manage this document and update it weekly or even daily.

LEARN ABOUT AGENCY TRAINING PROGRAMS

A growing number of the larger advertising agencies are creating large-scale training programs for their account management and media services departments. These intensive, highly competitive programs are an invaluable experience for anyone who wants to work on the business side of the industry. Applying for them means facing a rigorous slew of interviews and tests, but if you are accepted, you'll have the satisfaction of knowing that you are going to be groomed for a full-time position upon successful completion.

The Ogilvy Associates Program, for example, hires employees fresh out of college to participate in a rotation curriculum. During their three rotations, associates work with different clients, job roles, and teams. If you know you love account management, you can try working with clients in three different product areas. If you're not sure of the exact role you want, you can try out a rotation in media, another in account management, and another in research.

These programs teach everything that goes into creating a successful campaign. Some agencies bring in actual clients (often nonprofit organizations) and develop peer teams to create ad campaigns. Many of these programs include weekly luncheons and lectures with senior execs, big team projects, and collaborative presentations on the advertising process.

Some programs will set you up with an official mentor who will answer your questions and give you valuable advice. You'll learn the company policies and procedures for hiring, training, and developing employees. And unless you're a complete hermit, you'll forge some solid friendships, giving you a group of peers to commiserate with when you're all entry-level lackeys and reminisce with when you're all powerful senior execs. Participation usually means extra hours at the office. However, these programs are a great opportunity to gain invaluable skills and get quality face time with senior executives with whom a junior employee would normally never interact.

❝ The Ogilvy Associates Program has grown tremendously over the last few years and is the best entrée into the business. It allows you to actually experience daily life in different departments and then choose the department you want to stay in after the year is over. It's an incredible opportunity to gain experience and break into areas of the business that typically don't take entry-level employees. For me, it opened the door to strategic planning, a department that I could never have gotten into right out of college since I had neither work experience nor a master's degree."

—**Radhika Dewan,** Account Planner
Ogilvy & Mather

Areas of Training

In a training program, you can expect to cover the following.

- **Campaign strategy:** You will become familiar with all of the work that goes into planning and running an ad campaign, from detailed analysis of the competitive landscape to strategic discussions about launch dates, target audiences, and seasonality. You'll learn what goes into creating a media plan and see the analytical and mathematical side of figuring out where to place the ads.

- **Presentations:** Getting a client to sign off on a campaign and media buy requires not only a great idea, but also a killer presentation. When a client buys into a concept, he is also buying into your team and your agency. Training programs will give you the polished presentation skills that will allow you to deliver a message that's coherent and compelling.

- **Leadership development:** Most 20-year-old interns don't get to manage the creative process or write the media plan for a pitch to the San Diego Zoo. But many of these training programs hand their employees the reins to one of the agency's pro bono campaign accounts. The clients get a free ad idea and you get a great experience: Everybody wins. Managing a process like this will be intense, but you will emerge from it confident in your skills and ready to take on new challenges.

Training programs have benefits that standard internships do not. Still, the intense and rigorous instruction isn't for everyone. Think carefully about the kind of experience you want. Being the sole intern on a team will give you a better sense of what life is really like in the trenches. You'll see what typical ad agency employees experience day in and day out, and you'll get an in-depth perspective on one team and one aspect of the job. However, if you prefer a broader focus or if you want to be groomed for the advertising business fast track, a high-profile training program is a great option to consider.

GET AN INTERNSHIP

A great internship won't just fall into your lap. To get the really choice positions, you'll need to decide which companies to target and create a plan of action. Luckily, we just happen to have one here for you! You can thank us later.

Figuring Out Where You Want to Be

You'll want to consider a number of options: Should you use this as a chance to try a new position? Apply to your dream company? Go for the most glamorous position you can find? Stay open to applying for internships in lots of different settings, categories, and maybe even cities. And definitely think about the pros and cons of working at a small or large agency.

Notable advertising internship programs

Arnold Worldwide (arnoldworldwide.com)

Hill Holliday (hhcc.com)

Multicultural Advertising Training Program (MAT) (matprogram.org)

TBWA/Chiat/Day (tbwachiat.com)

The Advertising Club (theadvertisingclub. org)

Switching it up

If you're a college student, you may have a few summers to intern. Use these opportunities wisely. You could work for a large agency one summer and a small boutique the next, or you could pick one company and aim to intern there for multiple summers to really solidify the connection.

A small company or boutique will expose you to more aspects of the business and may lead to more interesting responsibilities. However, smaller agencies may not have room to hire you after you graduate. Also, the name of a smaller company on your résumé may be less powerful than the name of a bigger and better-known company.

Bigger agencies often offer more organized internships or even full-fledged training programs, providing structure and access to meaningful projects. However, they don't offer as much day-to-day exposure to senior execs and high-level planning processes. You may find that all the lectures you attend and group projects you participate in leave you with less time to help out around the office. Bigger companies may offer perks such as housing, field trips, rotation between departments, and preferential interviewing for full-time positions down the line. However, they can feel stuffy and formal. Some people don't enjoy working in a corporate environment, where there may be thousands of people in the building and as many as 20 on a team.

Europe, here I come!

Every company needs advertising, no matter where in the world it is. If you're looking for a summer adventure, why not head to London, an advertising mecca? Here are a few questions to consider before you reach for your passport.

- Does the agency hire foreign interns?

- What kinds of government visas and work permits are required?

- Is housing and cost of living affordable?

- Would you get lonely if you were away for an entire summer?

- Would the timing work out for school?

- Will this hurt your chances of finding a job back home?

Talking with Others

People love to talk about themselves and their experiences. Before committing to an entire summer at a particular ad agency, connect with some students who have already completed internships there.

Your contacts, particularly fellow students who have recently completed their own internship, will give you a more current and comprehensive, not to mention candid, depiction of their experiences. Want to know how much money you'll really earn during the summer? How much grunt work you'll be doing? What the office culture is really like? What to expect in the way of treatment and consideration? Go right ahead and ask. Most people will be happy to give you a straight answer to all of your questions. Some good questions to ask former interns include:

- Was your internship part of an established program, or was it a stand-alone position?
- What was your team like? How many people did you work with? What was the social dynamic like?
- How was your boss? Did you have to report to more than one person?
- What kind of work did you do? Did your boss(es) give you any meaningful and interesting projects, or was it mostly busywork?
- How was the office atmosphere? Did your team routinely work long hours?
- Did you get a chance to interact with people in full-time entry-level positions? Did their roles seem interesting and appealing to you?
- Did you have a particularly good or bad experience? Did it match up with your expectations?
- What were the best and worst aspects of the internship?
- Were you paid? How did you survive on your tight budget?
- Is there anything you wish you had known going in?
- Any regrets? Do you wish you would have done something different with your summer?
- What should I look for in an internship? What should I avoid?

Be wary of people who brag about how glamorous their experience was and how much face time they had with Mr. CEO—they're probably exaggerating. Be realistic in your expectations. A good internship can be an exciting, eye-opening experience that introduces you to lots of great people, but chances are, you'll get more face time with Mr. Copy Machine and Miss Scanner.

Frank answers to your questions will be really helpful as you determine which internships to look into or whether to pursue an internship at all. After all, your summers are precious. You want to lay the groundwork for a successful career, but you also want to get the most out of it, including a little relaxation.

Application Timeline

If you hope to get an internship by calling up Mediavest's human resources department on the first day of summer vacation, good luck. Serious planning is a must if you want to land an internship, particularly if you have your heart set on a specific program. Deadlines for the most competitive internships fall as early as February. Get the ball rolling early so that you have enough time to pull together a lengthy application, writing samples, and a recommendation or two.

Here's a typical timeline for preparing your applications. It's designed for college seniors but can be adapted for any intern hopefuls. Dates will vary depending on the specific program you're looking at, so while this may be a good guide, make sure you have exact dates for the agencies you're looking at.

FALL SEMESTER (SEPTEMBER–NOVEMBER)
- Update your résumé.
- Talk to other students about their internship experiences.
- Begin researching companies where you might like to intern.

WINTER VACATION
- Meet with your career center advisors to get advice on applying and information about specific companies and internship programs.
- If you're gunning for a creative role, get crackin' on your portfolio.
- Research the agencies and programs that interest you.
- Practice your interview skills.
- Create a spreadsheet like the one on the next page to keep track of opportunities, contact info, and deadlines.

SPRING SEMESTER (FEBRUARY–APRIL)
- Finalize your résumé.
- Finalize your portfolio and writing samples.

SAMPLE INTERNSHIP TRACKING SHEET

Date	Company	Contact Name	Contact Info	Activity	Next Step
1/26	Winter career fair	Amanda Schwartz	aschwartz@college.edu	Résumé review	Thank-you note
1/30	N/A	Prof. Dewall	dewall@college.edu	Asked for letter of rec	Follow up/thanks
2/7	MindShare	Jenna Ye class '00	(917) 555-8553; jenye@mindshareco.com	Informational phone call	Send résumé
2/15	Career center	Stacy Wall	Meeting to discuss internship possibilities	She called!	Call 3/25
2/22	Dynamite Agency	HR dept.	hr@dynamite.com	Sent résumé	Follow up
2/26	Dynamite Agency	Angela Polik	apolik@dynamite.com	Called to set up interview!	Interview, 3/10
3/5	Digitas	Kasey L.	(212) 555-6666	Met at event	Send res
3/10	Dynamite Agency	Angela Polik	See 2/26	Had interview!!!!	Thank-you note

- Ask faculty members and former employers for letters of recommendation, if you need them.
- Attend internship fairs hosted by your school or by outside companies.
- Put any online research into high gear.
- Apply, apply, apply.
- Have a great interview (or two, or nine . . .).
- Write thank-you notes.
- Work on your coffee making!

Plan ahead

Agencies that have single-intern programs are generally open to hiring interns all year round and are flexible about start and end dates. Larger programs have set application dates and more rigid schedules. They also get tons of applicants and are less likely to work around your personal schedule. If your school year ends late or you have a three-week vacation planned for the middle of the summer, it's wise to ask around before putting all your energy into getting in at a larger agency.

Finding and Applying for Internships

To find an internship, take full advantage of your personal and professional contacts. Talk to everyone. You never know who has a well-placed friend or relative. In addition, be a thorough and dogged researcher. Use everything from Google to your career center to your favorite industry magazines to dig up leads.

- **Network.** Tell your parents, faculty members, and the people you meet at career fairs and networking events that you're looking for an internship in advertising. Get their contact info and follow up.

- **Use school resources.** College career centers have job counselors, bulletin boards, and internship and career fairs that are usually open to current students and recent alums. Many school career centers also have subscriptions to job-posting sites and access to services such as monster.com, careerbuilder.com, and hotjobs.yahoo.com. Employers may contact

Many companies require you to get school credit for your internship. If you aren't currently enrolled in school or your school doesn't give credit for internships, you may not be eligible. Check the company's policy to avoid disappointment.

schools directly for referrals, so make sure to let professors and career counselors know that you're available and looking for work.

- **Rely on alumni associations.** Many schools keep detailed records of their alumni's contact info and places of employment. Find out if your school has an active alumni association or mentoring program that allows current students and recent grads to connect with alumni in their area of interest. It never hurts to contact someone who graduated from your school and now has a great advertising job or connection to the industry. If your school holds regional alumni mixers, attend, be charming and professional, and get the word out.

- **Subscribe to the trades.** *AdAge* and *Adweek* often list internships. Both magazines have subscription websites that may allow you to get info more quickly and beat the rest of the application crowd.

- **Go online.** Advertising internships are all over the Internet. Individual companies often post opportunities on their websites. Find further intern listings on sites such as Monster or Craigslist or have subscription services send targeted postings directly to you.

- **Put yourself out there—frequently.** You may be the best candidate ever to apply for an internship, but the reality is that hardly anyone gets the first job he or she applies for. Cast your net wide! Apply for lots of positions and don't get discouraged by rejection. It may take over a month for a company to set up an interview, so don't wait to hear from one company before you apply to another. Even if your dream internship doesn't materialize, applying for lots of positions will help you make contacts and get exposure to many companies.

- **Create your own internship.** If there are one or two agencies that you're just dying to work for, it's okay to focus your energies. Check out their websites regularly, pore over their ads, and keep up-to-date with their major news. Find out specific names of the people you'd like to work with and send them a brief, enthusiastic email explaining why you'd love to intern at their agency. Toss in a reference to one of their recent ads for good measure. If you need to go no holds barred,

Recommended websites

- advertising internships. net

- internship programs.com

- internshipslistings. com

- jobsearchsite.com

- craigslist.org

Interning, postgrad

Interning isn't just for college students anymore. Increasingly, recent grads are interning as a way to get their foot in the door. "Wait a second," you say. "I just finished four years of school! I'm ready for a real job!" We know. But it's a competitive job market out there. Taking a stand against postgrad internships probably won't help you; it will just ensure that the full-time jobs go to whoever *was* willing to soldier through that unpaid internship. Especially if you're lacking in industry experience, a postgrad internship is a great way to beef up your résumé while networking your way into full-time employment. As an added bonus, some companies even prefer recent grads as interns, since they won't be running back to school in three months and can merge seamlessly into a full-time position if it works out.

consider tapping a faculty member or career counselor for a letter of recommendation. Creatives should put together a mini-portfolio and send it along with their application. Keep in mind, there's a fine line between salesmanship and stalking: Keep all of your correspondence courteous and professional.

- **Follow the three cardinal rules of applications.** These rules are straightforward, but you'd be surprised at how many people disregard them:

    1. Meet the minimum qualifications.
    2. Follow the directions *exactly* as posted.
    3. Submit your application on time.

- **Don't be a pest.** If you really want an internship at Amalgamated and they haven't contacted you since your interview, send an email reiterating how much you enjoyed meeting them and what you have to offer them. If you still don't hear back, send a follow-up a week later. If you don't get a response, stop contacting them. They're either not interested or have a good reason for slowing down the process. If you're still in the running, appearing desperate or annoying will hurt your chances.

66 To prepare for my internship interview, I asked people that I knew in the industry what interview questions I might get. I made a list, wrote out answers, and practiced giving them in a very comfortable and friendly manner so they didn't seem rehearsed! Also, I looked up the company's website and read through it, looked at their clients' websites, and researched what was currently going on in the industry. Then I looked at certain advertisements so that I could say how I felt about them."

—**Brooke Firchow,** Assistant Account Executive
DDB

Comparing Opportunities

With some luck—and a bit of skill—you might be offered several internships. If you find yourself in this enviable position, consider the following as you determine the lucky winner.

- **The boss and the crew:** In organized internships, someone is specifically assigned to serve as your mentor. This person guides you, answers your questions, and introduces you to the important people in other departments. Having a mentor is great; having a kind, generous mentor is even better. You could be working on an award-winning campaign, but if your boss doesn't teach you anything, your experience won't be that valuable.

- **The work they've done:** Look at the different companies' portfolios. Identify the company whose client list best matches your interests. If you love most of the work created by a particular agency, you're more likely to enjoy your internship experience and leave it in a better position for a career you'll love.

- **Convenience and money:** Location matters. So does eating. Are you going to need three modes of transportation and a two-hour commute to get to work each day? Very few companies provide housing for interns, so if you have to go to another city to accept the position, will you be able to find an affordable place to stay that doesn't require a black belt and a bucket of mace? And if the internship is low or unpaid, will you be able to make it all summer without having to sell body parts for food?

- **Your long-term goals:** If you have a good idea of where you want to end up, get on the right path now. If you see yourself on the business end of advertising, your internship should involve some media planning or account managing. If you know that you ultimately want to work for a big pharma client, try working at an agency that handles those accounts. If your choice is between interning at a huge agency or a smaller boutique, decide which makes more sense for you and your long-term career plans. If you didn't land a position at your dream company, seek out a place with a similar standing so that you're more competitive next time around.

Perkfection

The offices of small boutique agency la comunidad in Miami and Buenos Aires aren't really offices at all. They're houses. *Adweek*'s Marketing y Medios 2006 Hispanic Advertising Agency of the Year works its creative magic from the confines of two beautiful homes, each complete with a pool and some well-placed hammocks, lending a comfortable family-like feel to the atmosphere. The intention is clear, as stated on la comu's website: "The office is no longer 'at your desk at 9, go home at 5, and eat something in between.' Routine is the enemy."

At the Paris offices of DDB, it's reported that employees can choose to leave work and grab a beer at any time if they're having a really bad day. And common perks at almost any agency include tons of free products lying around the office, a décor that's interesting if nothing else, great (and frequent!) happy hours, and wild holiday parties.

- **The intangibles:** Sometimes fringe benefits make all the difference. Free parking and a cafeteria that serves sushi may tip the balance for you. Maybe you can't pass up the chance to work at a hip, lively New York office. Or after visiting, you were struck with the appealing vision of yourself at that company in 15 years. You want to work at a place that excites you, and bragging about your internship can go far toward erasing the pain of an empty wallet.

SUCCEED AS AN INTERN (OR NOT)

Congratulations! You've landed your internship. Throw a party, call your mom, buy a new outfit. Then focus your energies on doing a terrific job so they'll ask you back. Here are the bona fide rules for making the most of your time.

10 Ways to Impress Your Employer

1. **Show up.** Be there on time and ready to work. Dress appropriately, which means observing what other people are wearing and matching them.

2. **Be professional, polite, and courteous.** This goes for everyone, from the janitors and receptionists to the directors and CEO.

3. **Listen and absorb.** There's a lot going on and you're there to learn it, so pay attention.

4. **Smile.** Cheerfully accept all assignments—even the gofer stuff like making coffee, running errands, or filing samples.

5. **Participate when asked.** Take advantage of opportunities to offer your opinion, but don't feel that you need to voice your thoughts all the time.

6. **Be proactive.** Don't just sit around and wait for meaningful work to come your way. Ask how you can help out and promptly tell your supervisor when you're finished with an assignment and ready to take on new ones.

7. **Limit lunch to lunchtime.** And always keep your personal business out of the workplace.

8. **Stay committed.** Don't leave two weeks early because you've got too much schoolwork or your family's going on vacation to Mexico.

9. **Ask questions.** And not just when you don't understand something. Show your interest by asking questions about how things really work. And whenever you have the opportunity, meet with people outside your team to learn more.

10. **Find a mentor.** If the company doesn't assign you someone to work with directly, seek one out on your own.

10 Ways to Lose Your Internship (and Any Chance of Working for the Company in the Future!)

1. **Cry.** No matter how harshly you're criticized, don't do it. You'll need thick skin to succeed in this business. If you absolutely must shed a few, head to the nearest bathroom stall or go for a walk around the block. Never cry at your desk or in a meeting.

2. **Arrive late.** Figure out the traffic patterns and subway schedules, whatever you need to do to be on time. Find out when your boss gets in and aim to arrive earlier than she does.

3. **Have an attitude.** Your employer can tell when you're silently fuming, thinking, "I am way too educated to be wasting my time with this nonsense!"

4. **Wait until mid-morning to call in sick.** And don't call in sick more than once, unless it's physically impossible to haul your body into work.

5. **Take photos of the work you're doing (even your own!) without permission.** And don't even think about starting a "My First Internship" blog.

6. **Take anything home with you.** Ad agencies are chock full of really cool stuff. Leave it there. Don't be tempted to take home a goody or two, expecting that no one will notice.

7. **Question your superiors.** Remember you're there to learn from them.

8. **Badmouth anyone in your company or a competing one, even if you hear others doing it.** You never want to be known as the loose-lipped office gossip.

9. **Be embarrassed to admit that you don't understand something.** Your boss would much rather explain it again than have you screw it up completely.

10. **Leave an internship two days (or two weeks) after starting because you've found a better one.** This portends some permanent bridge burning, which means alienating a potential future employer (or colleague). The industry is small, and you're likely to run into all these people again.

EXPLORE ALTERNATIVES TO INTERNING

If you're not sure that you want to spend your summer as an intern or if none of your interning options seems right, there are plenty of other good opportunities out there that will allow you to learn about the advertising industry.

- **Work in retail.** Working in retail isn't just a good way to make a chunk of spending money; it's also a great way to get to know the ins and outs of consumerism. You'll see firsthand how companies measure success and determine what their target audience is. You'll see which ads draw people to the stores and which seasons are most important for a killer campaign. Perhaps most important, you'll interact with customers, learn how to appease them when they're dissatisfied, discuss their loves and hates, and respond directly to their feedback. An understanding of your client's product and how the customer approaches it are valuable tools when it comes time to create your own ad campaigns.

- **Work at a magazine or web publication.** You can gain valuable experience interning at a publication, print or online, even if it's not directly related to advertising. An internship with an editorial department will help you develop the ability to write clearly and concisely for a specific audience, which will come in handy when working on creative briefs or ad copy. You'll also develop an understanding of advertising from the perspective of the media representative selling space. Be warned, though: Internships in this field are just as coveted and difficult to snag as ad agency internships. If you have a strong writing background and a strong ad background, you could be a very competitive candidate, but you'll need to plan out your steps.

- **Take a class.** This could be the perfect time to brush up on a few skills or take the graphic design or writing course that could give you the competitive edge. Consider taking a summer class at a specialized school, where you might be able to network with professors or gain access to alumni listings.

- **Work at school.** Many universities offer summer courses for high school students. If you're a college student and you'll be near campus for the summer, look into becoming a teacher's assistant. This is a particularly good option if you need to take summer classes, since TAs often enjoy deeply discounted or waived tuition. Some programs may even provide housing.

- **Do administrative work.** If you can't land your dream internship, get your foot in the door by doing administrative work at an agency. As a temp or receptionist, you're in a good position to meet many people and start building up your contact list. This may seem a little roundabout, but many bosses develop strong relationships with great administrative assistants and are happy to promote them or provide them with recommendations. Admin work will also give you a useful overview of the way an agency works.

- **Volunteer.** Many organizations are begging for free help! Assist with advertising for a nonprofit, religious organization, or student group or consider volunteering your talents at a major ad industry event. The projects you work on as a volunteer may not be sexy and glamorous, but the experience will be important nonetheless.

Broadening your horizons

Inspiration can come from anywhere, so take advantage of every opportunity to broaden your horizons. If you're planning on traveling cross-country or overseas over summer vacation or after graduation, make it a research trip. Take your camera, your sketchbook, and a bag to collect the objects that captivate you. You might find inspiration for an ad campaign in the vast expanses of New Mexico or on the beaches of South Africa. As you travel, pay attention to unique methods of advertising, particularly on the street, and learn what sells in other regions and countries.

6

GETTING A JOB

You're almost there. You've been researching your fingers to the bone, networking like crazy, and interning your heart out. You're all set to knock 'em dead with some sharp attire, a killer résumé, and that never-say-die attitude. Now for the last piece of the equation: Getting a job. If you've done your homework, you're in good shape. Time to punch your ticket and get going with your career.

RESEARCH YOUR OPTIONS

Applying to 300 companies at once would be a waste of energy and a recipe for chaos. An effective search requires the talents of your inner party planner. Whittle down your guest list to just the VIPs: those companies that you would most like to work for. Everyone's VIP list is a little different. Maybe you want to work for the trendy company with hundreds of awards under its belt. Perhaps you prefer a small boutique or specialized agency that focuses on a particular niche in the market. Or maybe you're looking for a proven industry leader with some iconic brand names among its clientele. Your list may even include an assortment of all these options.

In truth, your VIP list will be in a state of continual flux as you find out about new hiring opportunities, discover new agencies, and refine your own desires as you learn more about the business. But even if you are applying for jobs online and juggling many applications at once, keep a list in mind of your three to five dream jobs.

In most departments, entry-level workers tend to get promoted within one or two years, leaving room for another class of future ad execs.

Finding Job Postings

Advertising jobs are always out there. Agencies win accounts and uncover new markets and media outlets on a daily basis. People in the industry are continually moving to higher positions or different departments within an agency or jumping from agency to agency or agency to client as new opportunities present themselves.

Most successful job searches come with a bit of sleuthing. The trick is to be ready to strike when these openings come up. Job openings will come at you from company websites, job search sites, official recruiters, and word of mouth. Here are a few things you can do to power up your search.

PUBLICATIONS

Read *AdAge* and *Adweek* religiously to see who is winning or losing client accounts and who might be in the position to hire. Keep up with who's being promoted or leaving for another firm, paving the way for others to move up and you to move in. Set aside time on a daily basis for your advertising news hour.

ONLINE JOB LISTINGS

Most companies post the latest openings or at the very least information about their hiring process. Make a daily practice of visiting the websites of companies you're most interested in. Check out organizations such as AAAA and AAF for their latest postings. Take advantage of your school's online job board, if one exists, to access jobs that might not be available to the general public. Also check out the large job posting websites listed below.

- **Mediabistro.com**
  Mediabistro.com lists job openings, runs articles written by industry insiders, and organizes cocktail hours and other networking events. It also posts industry gossip and news about where people are going, who has recently switched jobs, and who has been promoted.

- **Talent Zoo,** talentzoo.com
  Talent Zoo has many job postings for account management and creative services, both for ad agencies and for clients. *Forbes* magazine voted it one of the best media job-posting sites on the web.

- **Monster,** monster.com
  The leading job site on the net, Monster's broad variety of job listings includes a robust section on advertising and media.

- **Jobster.com**
  This Web 2.0 site connects thousands of job seekers to employers in virtually every industry.

- **Indeed.com**
  This meta-job posting site that searches most of the leading career sites and compiles data on open positions in one place.

ON-CAMPUS RECRUITING

Often larger ad agencies will send a recruiter to college campuses to host informational sessions and conduct interviews for full-time entry-level positions. Keep your ears open for news about upcoming sessions at your campus or others in your area. Recruiters can give you the lowdown on their company, the industry, and the types of jobs available to entry-level applicants. Meeting with them in person is a good way to enhance the connection. And interviews held on your campus afford you the opportunity of applying to multiple agency jobs without incurring traveling expenses.

WHAT WANTED ADS TELL YOU (AND WHAT THEY DON'T)

A job listing is meant to catch your eye and entice you to apply. It will usually give you the basics: title, location, general responsibilities, requisite years of experience or education, and where to send your résumé. It usually *won't* tell you how much the job pays or what the work environment is like. And it definitely won't tell you what kind of hours you'll have to work or whom you'll be working with. If the listing provides a company name (not all do!), you'd be wise to head straight to your sources and get the scoop. Why are they looking to hire for that position? Are they expanding, or did someone leave? Do they have a reputation as a good place to work? With a bit of due diligence, you'll get a better idea if this is the opportunity you want to pursue.

SAMPLE WANTED AD

Assistant Media Planner

Immediate opening with a major consumer product client team in the New York area.

RESPONSIBILITIES:
- Assist on projects to learn the techniques of media planning and account services and to ensure the successful development of clients' media plans.
- Learn key industry tools to contribute to and support the stages of plan development.
- Manage daily general administrative tasks for the team and assist with client meeting preparation by providing administrative support for media planners.
- Assist in researching, buying, and executing print media.
- Update monthly competitive template and complete client competitive requests.
- Assist planner with developing flowcharts on delivery analysis and budget summaries.
- Update key internal documents and weekly status reports.
- Attend team conference calls/meetings and keep abreast of newsworthy, relevant issues affecting the advertising industry, as well as the specific brand category.
- Work with team to develop and present competitive/state of business analysis.

REQUIREMENTS:
- Bachelor's degree (coursework in media, advertising, or marketing a plus).
- Must be self-sufficient, a quick learner, and a creative thinker.
- Strong problem-solving skills and determination to get the job done.
- Effective organizational skills and ability to prioritize.
- Excellent communication and writing skills.
- Mastery of basic MS Office applications, specifically Excel and PowerPoint.
- Exposure to research tools such as IMS, MediaTools, and Adviews is a plus.

Interested parties should send their résumé and cover letter to admin@adgold.com.

Researching Specific Companies

Before you customize your résumé, apply for a job, or go in for an interview, find out as much as possible about your potential employer. Doing so will help you weed out companies that are not a good fit for you. And it will show the people at companies you *do* match with that you care enough to do your homework. Here are a few of the best ways to research companies.

- **Visit the company's website.** What better way to learn about a company than to hear what they say about themselves? Most company websites have a mission statement, company philosophy, listings of historic work, and recent awards and news. Some include detailed information such as company org charts, financial statements, and major investors and shareholders. Look for information about head executives, managers, and directors. And let the site speak for itself: Pay attention to the design to get a sense of the company's style and creative direction.

- **Pay attention to the ads.** A key aspect to researching a company is figuring out who their clients are and what campaigns they're involved in. Sounds obvious, right? But if you're interviewing with Cramer and Krasselt and know nothing about their award-winning "Working with monkeys" campaign, chances are you can kiss that job goodbye. Know your potential employer's current campaign for each major brand, as well as significant campaigns from the past. To go above and beyond, analyze some ads run by major competitors and come up with opinions on their strengths and weaknesses.

- **Read the industry resources.** *The* Advertising Age *Encyclopedia of Advertising,* the Red Book, the AAAA, and the AAF: These are all great places for news and information on virtually every agency, large or small. If a company's not listed somewhere in one of these, chances are it's not worth knowing about . . . yet.

- **Fine-tune your search engines.** Your favorite search engines are always handy for some quick research. But there is an art to using them. Instead of checking daily or weekly for updates on the industry and leading agencies, sign up for an RSS feed and let Google do all the work for you! Provide a few key words (such as the names of specific agencies or fields you're interested in), and you'll receive a daily email with news containing those key words.

PUT YOUR NETWORK TO USE

Advertising is a business built on connections, and you'll find this to be true when you search for your first job . . . and your second, third, and fourth. A lead from someone within a company can be a huge advantage. Chances are, word won't have been made public, so your competition will be limited. Also, a recommendation from an insider gives you instant cred.

So now it's time to get in touch with all those contacts you've been making. Approach each person with a simple eye-catching email that politely requests a response. A passive or evasive message won't inspire anyone to action, so be direct.

Keep track of all the responses you get and write down the next step you plan to take. Note who needs a follow-up, who's due for a gentle reminder in the next week, and who should be dropped from your list altogether.

If you don't hear back in a week, don't jump to the conclusion that they want nothing to do with you. It's possible that your emails are getting buried in an overburdened in-box. Send a follow-up email or call to say a friendly hello and ask your contact if she received your email. Acknowledge in your message that she must be busy. Don't be too pushy and keep any defensive tendencies in check. If you contact someone three times and she doesn't respond, let it go.

66 Last time I counted, 85 percent of our new advertising/sales team hires came from employee referrals and word-of-mouth recommendations . . . although we interview a good mix of candidates from many different sources."

—**Meagan Marks,** Senior Recruiter
Facebook

Building Up Your Network

The more people you know, the more likely you are to be one of those personal referrals rather than one of the desperate masses emailing their résumé to an unknown human resources director. As you continue your job search, also continue your networking. Here are some of the places you should be looking.

- **Internships:** As an intern, you interact with many people beyond your supervisor. Get to know the other members of your department and those working in other departments. You don't have to invite them to dinner, but a friendly greeting in passing or at company events will help to keep you on the radar. And build a relationship with the human resources department. When word of a new opening comes down, you want to be in position to jump right on it. Other interns will also be able to steer you to the new openings.

- **Professors:** Cultivate your relationships with your professors. Even if your professor isn't working at an agency himself, he probably has tons of friends who are. If your professor has written books or made appearances, it is all the more likely that he has connections to people in media, marketing, and advertising.

- **On-campus career centers:** Your school has a vested interest in seeing that you find a job. They look good if you look good. Many schools will match you up with a career counselor who can help you prepare your résumé and offer you advice on conducting your search. In many cases, these counselors will have contacts either in the field you want or at recruiting agencies in the city you're interested in. The catch is that there are probably hundreds of students in the same boat as you, all of whom want their résumés passed along. Work at maintaining a relationship with your counselor so that you're at the top of their list when something comes up.

A word on advertising industry centers

If you're still in school, you're probably thinking a lot about where you'll live after that magical graduation day. Advertising agencies are clustered primarily in New York City, Chicago, Los Angeles, and San Francisco. As is usually the case, more jobs are available in big cities, which means greater options and more opportunities (and fiercer competition!), but you can find terrific jobs in advertising almost anywhere in the country. For example, Fallon, an international ad agency that works with Citibank and other major brands, has offices in Minneapolis. Head to Washington, D.C., for agencies that specialize in political advertising or out to Seattle to work at Avenue A, one of the leading agencies in interactive media.

If you're curious about what life would be like in a particular city, talk to the people who have lived there, both in advertising and in other lines of work. Chat with people who have visited that city for fun or business. Check out sites like Craigslist and CitySearch for restaurant and event listings and for a taste of the local flavor. Research the social scene for young people. It's really important to be happy with your job, but it's even more important to be happy with the city where you live.

With a little luck, you'll be able to match up the agencies that have created your favorite ads with the city or cities you would like to call home for the next few years (and possibly longer).

- **Freelancing:** Freelancing is a great way to make contacts in the industry. Although the majority of these opportunities are on the creative side, there are options for just about anyone looking to get into advertising. The work isn't guaranteed. And you may find it necessary to pick up some temp work here and there to keep food on your table, but this can be a great chance to get your feet wet, put your name out there, and make valuable contacts.

- **Alumni:** Ask the alumni office about how to hook up with other alumni in the advertising industry. Your college probably has an online newsletter, a bulletin board, or even an alumni mentor program. If someone from your college has a great job at an ad agency in a place you want to live, use them to get your foot in the door. Prepare for some chatting when you call someone up; many alums love to talk about their chosen industry with interested young people.

As you focus your job search, you'll start to see every occasion as an opportunity to meet new people and expand your network. Don't forget, networking is something you can do at social as well as professional events. Next time you show up at a party, don't let yourself cling to the two people you walked in with. Instead, strike up a conversation with at least three other people. Ask for their business card or contact info. If you're shy by nature, consider enlisting a gregarious friend who will drag you out from behind your plate of crudités.

DISCUSSING PREREQUISITES

Doing simple research as you begin the interview process will save you time and help you get comfortable with your own skill set and experience. You don't want to set your heart on a media-planning role, get halfway through the interview process, and learn that the interviewer wants to know about your work in a statistics class you never took.

To prevent any surprises, find now what is expected in your desired field. Does the job you are applying for typically call for two years of previous agency experience? Does the research role require three courses in statistics? Does the specialized healthcare agency look for a background in pharma and medicine?

Use your contacts to help fill in the details. Ask people in senior roles what they would look for in a candidate. And when you're looking at job postings, keep track of the typical background and prerequisites the agencies are looking for. If you feel you're deficient in a particular area, find out what you can do to fill in the gap. After all, you may be able to fudge "extensive PowerPoint skills" by completing a 45-minute demo, but there's no way you'll be able to fake an advanced course in media planning.

APPLY

You can have the best grades, the most relevant experience, and a list of contacts to rival the CEO of Omnicom, but none of it will matter unless people know that you're looking for a job. Fear of rejection can be powerful, but it's crucial that you overcome it. The more you reach out, the easier it will become, and the more confident you'll be in your ability to pick up the phone and pitch yourself as a stellar candidate to somebody you've never met. Here are a few tips to follow when applying for an opening.

- **Be direct.** When making a cold call (or sending a cold email), don't beat around the bush in asking about job openings. Keep your message concise, confident, and straightforward. If you sound timid, stumble over words, or ramble on and on, you risk annoying your contact and discouraging him from helping you.

- **Take charge.** If you're working with a recruiting agency, it will send out your résumé for you. Your job is to explain exactly what position you want and exactly what type of company you want to work for—or, if you're undecided, to explain your reasons. If you don't give a clear idea of your specific goals and interests, you may find yourself sitting through many fruitless interviews. Be honest and then sit back and let the recruiter do her job.

- **Mimic their style.** If someone responds to you by saying, "Please send your résumé," don't reply with a gusher of gratitude and a two-page explanation of why you're perfect for the job. Be equally brief. If they ask you for a bit of explanation, fire away, but make your message focused. And keep the thanks in check: Think sincere, not sappy.

- **Follow directions.** When submitting a written or online application, follow the directions *exactly*. Adhering to instructions, even those that seem unimportant, could mean the difference between getting an interview and getting tossed in the recycling bin. If they want two writing samples, send two writing samples, not one or three. Make sure you're attaching documents in the proper format or not at all if they want everything in the body of an email. And most important, meet the deadline.

The art of cold emailing

Cold emailing is a bit of a crapshoot. You have just a few seconds to convince the recipient to open and read your message rather than delete it. Even the best efforts won't always work, but here are some suggestions to make those few seconds count.

- **Choose your subject line wisely.** If you write "looking for a job," you may as well ask the recipient to hit delete. State your exact objective and the specific position you want.

- **Include a compelling cover letter.** Don't open with "To whom it may concern." Address a specific person by name. Then devote one sentence to introducing yourself, one to explaining how you heard about the position, one to summarizing how you meet the needs of the employer, and one to encouraging the recipient to look at your résumé.

- **Put your résumé in the body of the email.** In this age of virus proliferation, not many people will open an attachment from an unknown person (and depending on protection software, it might not even make it through). Put your résumé right in the message.

- **Make sure your résumé is formatted.** Unorganized or indecipherable résumés aren't much good to anyone. Make sure your résumé looks good on all computers and email systems. Send a test run to yourself or a friend.

- **Send wisely.** If a company requests more information or samples from you, send something relevant to the types of work you'll be doing. Don't send a television commercial reel if the job is all print! And if you're applying for a position that focuses on emerging online media, don't send something that's three years old. When you're sending, include an electronic version whenever possible so that the recipient can easily share your sample with others.

- **Send often.** It's always a good idea to send out lots of résumés. If you're already sending out one, spend a few extra minutes to see if there are any other postings up that you can apply to. The most awful that could happen is that *everyone* will be interested, and you'll find yourself with 100 interviews to choose between. Things could be worse.

Never mail an original or anything so valuable to you that you would be crushed if you never saw it again.

RECRUITERS

You might consider working with an executive search firm or recruiter to help locate job opportunities. Recruiters work with companies to find suitable candidates for open positions. This is a mutually beneficial arrangement for all parties, since the recruiter is only paid when you get a job (and it's usually your new employer that will pay them). Steer clear of recruiters that require money from you up front or ask you to sign an exclusive contract barring you from working with another service. And if repeated calls or emails from you go unanswered, it's probably an indication that the recruiter is not completely reliable. Although neither the authors nor publishers of this book endorse any of these services, here are some of the better-known firms in the industry.

Recruiters have reputations too. Ask around or pose the question on a campus chat board. Try to get more than one opinion!

- **Adecco Creative,** adeccocreative.com
  A subdivision of the international recruiter Adecco, this group was founded not too long ago as a creative services provider. It caters to many markets, including advertising, public relations, and publishing. This is a great source of work for prospective art directors and copywriters.

- **Greenberg Kirshenbaum,** greenbergkirshenbaum.com
  A New York–based recruitment firm that locates permanent and freelance opportunities for creative talent in advertising and new media agencies worldwide.

- **Lynne Palmer Executive Recruitment,** lynnepalmerinc.com
  Since 1964, this agency has been placing qualified people into jobs throughout marketing and media industries. Look here for open creative, sales, account manager, public relations, and media positions at agencies nationwide.

- **Ribolow Associates,** ribolow.com
  This recruiting agency specializes in the advertising and publishing industries. Its sister company, Ribolow Staffing Services, also provides temporary work for professionals in transition.

Cover Letters

Most people are thrown into fits at the prospect of writing the dreaded cover letter. "How do I convey enthusiasm without sounding over the top and insincere? How do I communicate my strengths and skills without coming across as totally arrogant and obnoxious? What can I say in two or three paragraphs that will make someone think, 'Wow, we've just *got* to bring this kid in for an interview'?"

Breathe. It's not as bad as you think. Envision your cover letter as a chance to explain yourself with more personality than the outline of your résumé allows. Your cover letter is an opportunity to use your own words to demonstrate why you should be working for this specific company in this specific field. It doesn't have to be Pulitzer Prize–winning stuff; it just has to have a straightforward introduction, a few appealing items about yourself, and a clinching closer.

Read over the sample cover letter on the next page and the corresponding tips that follow.

1. **Write to a specific person.** Your cover letter is more likely to get noticed if you address it to a specific person rather than "HR Department." And be sure to take the time to get the name right.

SAMPLE COVER LETTER

Jane Q. Student
555 Baron Dr.
Anywheresville, CT 05455
639-555-1220

April 10, 2007

(1) Ms. Ida Hiredu
DDB Worldwide
674 Midtown Manhattan
East Side, NY 55555

(2) Dear Ms. Hiredu,

(3) I was referred to you by Joseph Byrne, an account supervisor on the Hershey
(4) account. I am a senior majoring in psychology and media, and I am currently
looking for an assistant account executive position after graduation this
coming May. Mr. Byrne informed me of an opening on the Hershey account
management team, and it sounds perfect for me. I have attached my résumé
for your review.

(5) I think you'll agree that my coursework and experiences make me an ideal
candidate. I recently completed my honors senior thesis on psychology and
online media, in which I analyze how people respond to different forms of
advertising on the Internet. In addition, I have completed specialized coursework
in emerging forms of marketing and am currently enrolled in a class titled
"Youth Marketing in the 21st Century." I have also spent the past two summers
volunteering in the marketing department for the Special Olympics, creating
direct-marketing materials to encourage corporate sponsorship.

(6) I am passionate about brand advertising, and Hershey would be exciting to
(7) work with. From the Hershey's mint "holiday kisses" campaign to the "How
do you eat your Reeses?" campaign, DDB has created a unique personality
for each of Hershey's best-selling products, an accomplishment I admire.

(8) As the most vocal advocate of my family's annual Hersheypark trips, I can't
tell you how exciting it would be to use my education and ability to market
your products. I am confident that my skills, enthusiasm, and passion would
benefit your company, and I look forward to speaking with you about the
opportunities that are available.

(9) I can be reached by email at janeq@geemail.com or by cell phone at (639) 555-1220.

Thank you,

JANE Q. STUDENT

Jane Q. Student

If you're not sure whether "Adrian Peterson" is a man or a woman, see if you can locate that person on Google or a social networking site such as MySpace or LinkedIn. Otherwise, you can always call the company and ask the receptionist. If you can't find the info you need, address the person with the acceptable but clunky "Dear Adrian Peterson," rather than risk offending her with the greeting "Dear Mr. Peterson."

2. **Keep it professional.** Your cover letter is not the place to display your natural quirkiness and deft wit. Leave that for your sample or interview. Don't address someone by his first name or nickname unless it's been established through a personal relationship. Use formal business letter format and maintain a proper tone. If you land an interview, the person you're talking with may set a more casual tone that you can match. Until then, keep it professional.

3. **Explain why you're writing.** Did someone within the company refer you? Are you responding to an online job listing? Did you attend an informational session or recruiting event through your school? Say exactly why you're writing.

4. **Provide your current status.** Whether you're graduating in three weeks and are heading straight to New York City, available as soon as school ends in six months, or currently working at another company in the same city, let your potential employer know your situation.

5. **Give them a reason to pick you.** What sets you apart from everyone else in the pool? Offer a recap of your major accomplishments without sounding too arrogant. You have a fine line to walk: This is not a time to be shy or flat, but neither is it a time to come across as a pompous jerk. Don't list every award you've won since second grade and every leadership position you've held from hall monitor on up. Mention your relevant experience and accomplishments, such as your award-winning senior thesis on marketing or your two summer internships at Saatchi & Saatchi.

6. **Give your reasons for picking them.** Your cover letter isn't a generic template. If potential employers suspect that you are sending the same letter to 50 companies, they'll be turned off. Convince them that you want to work at *their* company. Explain what you like about them, which of their key clients interest you, and which ad campaigns have influenced you.

7. **Show that you've done your research.** Demonstrate your knowledge and passion. Prove that you have gone above and beyond by researching the company and the state of the industry. Discuss related projects you've worked on that illustrate how with it you really are. Convince them that you're more prepared than any other applicant.

8. **Demonstrate that you belong.** Explain what makes you the right person for the job. Be clear and succinct and offer specific examples. Why are your experiences so valuable to the company? What skills do you possess that make you the best candidate? Let your inner salesperson loose and tell them exactly why you're the superstar they're looking for.

9. **Provide your contact info.** Let them know the best way to reach you. Provide a professional-sounding email address that you check regularly and a phone number where you're easily reachable in case they need to schedule an interview on short notice.

Timing is everything

Advertising jobs tend to fill quickly. When someone moves on to another agency, she needs to be replaced right away. If you're going to graduate from school in mid-May, start applying for jobs in late March or early April. Give yourself six to eight weeks for the interview process but not much more than that. Once you agree to take a position, your employer will want you to start soon. If you plan on traveling for the summer and starting work in September, you might be able to get an informational interview or two, but don't expect any job offers.

INTERVIEW

Interviewing can get expensive, and agencies won't usually cover your travel costs. Cut down on expenses by combining several interviews into a single trip.

You've cast your résumé out and gotten a bite. They've decided to invite you into their world to see if you'll fit. Take a deep breath. It's natural to be nervous, but remind yourself that this company wouldn't have asked you for an interview if they weren't excited about what you could offer. This is your chance to show what an intelligent, passionate, and charismatic person you are. It's your golden opportunity to wow them with the knowledge you've been collecting about the advertising industry as a whole and their company in particular.

Preparing for Your Interview

Preparation leads to confidence. Learning about the person who will be interviewing you is one of the most important ways to prep for your interview. Some companies' websites include employee bios. Otherwise, hit your online resources for the latest news.

If it's the night before your interview and you haven't done a lick of research, fear not. Some preparation time is better than none. Even doing just a few hours of research will give you the advantage over someone coming in cold. Here are a few last-minute preparation tips to help you look as if you spent the last few weeks getting ready.

- **Get a detailed job description.** Know exactly what is expected of you and what skills and relevant experiences to highlight.

- **Visit the company's website.** Make sure you can name key clients and talk fluently about creative material posted on their site.

- **Be up-to-date.** Get familiar with any recent press or major news about the company.

- **Prepare to talk about yourself.** You may want to practice by talking about your biggest achievements to a friend or even to yourself. It may seem a bit silly, but you'll sound poised and confident when you're talking to an interviewer.

Advice for the Big Day

Even the smallest errors can take the focus away from you and your qualifications. Avoiding interview faux pas may seem easy, but you'd be shocked by the number of people who scuttle their chances with silly mistakes. Following these pointers will allow the real you to shine through.

- **Arrive early.** There's no need to camp outside the front door the night before, but aim to arrive 10 to 15 minutes ahead of your scheduled interview time. Make sure you have good directions and know exactly how to get to the interview location. Leave yourself extra time to deal with traffic, far-flung parking lots, and confusing buildings. Factor in extra time for filling out paperwork, grabbing a drink of water, stopping by the restroom, or touching up your hair.

- **Dress professionally.** It may be the first and last time you wear formal business attire at an ad agency, but appropriate interview clothes (a suit for men and a suit or formal business outfit for women) shows that you respect your interviewer and the company. Most people in advertising wear jeans or trendy business casual, and you can too . . . after you've gotten the job.

- **Bring your supplies.** Come armed with extra copies of your résumé (on elegant, wrinkle-free paper), your portfolio with some leave-behind samples (if you're a creative), and a notepad and pen in case it seems appropriate to take notes.

- **Start strong.** When you are first introduced to your interviewer, look him in the eye as you say hello, extend your hand for a firm handshake, and thank him for meeting with you.

- **Say yes to water.** Many places will offer you a beverage. You should accept one and display your gracious manners with a polite thank-you. Your best bet is to stick with water. Other beverages can be tricky or dangerous—the caffeine and sugar in coffee, juice, tea, or soda could leave you jittery or upset a slightly nervous stomach. Water is also useful to have in case you develop a nervous hoarseness or a tickle in your throat, and it doesn't leave a trace in the event of a mishap.

- **Straighten up.** Nonverbal communication can reveal more than the words coming out of your mouth. Slouching in your chair will make you look tired and uninterested. An upright posture will demonstrate your energy and enthusiasm, and it'll keep you alert. It's a good idea to check out your posture in a mirror before the interview.

- **Give short, concise answers.** Nervousness and the desire to impress can lead you to some awkward rambling. But wordy and bumbling speech won't just confuse your interviewer, it'll cause her to tune out. Take a moment before you speak to compose your thoughts, and answer as directly and clearly as you can.

- **Get specific.** Rather than speaking in abstractions, provide examples of work you've done and accolades you've won. Talk about the awesome performance review from your summer internship or the killer grades you got on that marketing analysis project in school.

- **Move beyond school.** Talk about excellence you've achieved in extracurricular activities or work-related experiences. Companies like people who are well rounded. Your experiences show that you are a unique, hardworking, and ambitious person. This will also help spark an interesting conversation between you and your interviewer that lets you connect on a personal level.

66 Be yourself, be enthusiastic (not unctuous), talk, ask questions, try to get comfortable, smile, and don't overdress."

—**Jill Rothman,** Director of Production
JWT

Typical Interview Queries

Interviews follow some basic patterns. By anticipating what questions will be asked, you can keep relaxed and focused during the interview. Here are some typical questions that you should be ready to answer in your interview. Prepare your responses beforehand to avoid incoherence or, worse yet, silence. You may even want to rehearse your responses out loud the night before.

- ***Tell me about yourself.*** (Translation: What are the few most relevant things that I should know when assessing you for this job?) Start with why you're attracted to advertising and what brought you to this particular company. Don't discuss how you love the beach and the fabulous time you had your last trip to the Bahamas. Stay focused on topics related to the industry.

- ***Why do you want to go into advertising?*** (Translation: Why are you really here?) This should relate to your response to the first question but with more detail on what you like best about the industry or a personal anecdote about what inspired your interest in advertising. Be honest and don't spend your time coming up with an elaborate story that someone will see through in a second. And no matter how true it may be, "to make a lot of money" is almost never a good answer.

- ***Why do you want to work for us?*** (Translation: Prove to me that you know something about our company.) This is where all that research and networking pays off. Name-drop if someone who works at the company recommended you. Show your familiarity with the company's history, your awareness of recent events, and your take on the ads they've created. Express enthusiasm for the company and their clients and reinforce why you'd be a great fit.

- **What inspires you?** (Translation: Are you passionate enough to work crazy hours for not much money?) Tell the interviewer what makes you want to get up in the morning. How does this passion translate into a job at her company?

- **What is the best ad you've ever seen? What is the worst?** (Translation: How well do you understand the industry and how ads perform?) Be prepared to talk about ads that have genuinely excited you. Have a few examples ready from a range of product types and mediums. And whatever you do, make sure the company you're interviewing with didn't produce your "worst" example.

- **Tell us about your coursework and activities.** (Translation: Show me that this isn't just a whim.) If you've put it together well, your résumé should provide a good outline for your answer. Now it's time to fill in the details. Be ready with a thoughtful answer about your coursework and school activities that show you used your time in school for more than debt accumulation. Talk about relevant projects such as the marketing you've done for student groups or any heavy-duty research assignments. Stress anything for which you received honors or accolades.

- **Tell me about your internships.** (Translation: Show me that you used your time for education, not socializing.) Your interviewer wants to see that you're committed and passionate about the advertising world. Your experiences in an internship should reflect that enthusiasm. If you've never had an internship, spin the experiences you have had to stress your leadership abilities, teamwork skills, or willingness to work hard and learn a lot.

- **If you were a color, what would you be?** (Translation: Time to test your pulse.) Be on guard for oddball questions like this one. When an interviewer asks you to talk about the last book you read or what your favorite animal is, he really wants to see your personality and test your ability to think on your feet. You won't encounter this kind of question in every interview, and there's no real way to prepare an answer for something so random. But be warned that such questions may come up. The best advice is not to panic and have a little fun.

> **Now let's look at your portfolio**
>
> For creatives, potential employers count on your work to give them an idea of your abilities before you're invited in for an interview. Be prepared to go into your interview and watch as your interviewer pores over your portfolio, either complimenting you, remaining silent, or tearing it apart before your eyes. Don't take criticisms personally, and have the courage to defend your work in an appropriate manner. Take note of constructive critiques and make changes as necessary. Learning from these experiences is part of developing the thick skin every creative needs.

DO YOU HAVE ANY QUESTIONS?

Toward the end of the interview, you will inevitably be asked whether you have questions. The worst thing you can say is "no." It tells the interviewer that you haven't thought much about her company or your possible role in it. Some good questions to ask are, "How would you describe the company culture?" "What are the challenges facing your company/department?" "What are the typical prospects for advancement?" and, "Is there travel involved with this position?"

Use your judgment to decide how many questions you should ask and what types of questions are appropriate. Where possible, you want your questions to demonstrate that you were listening carefully during the interview. Phrasing your question as a follow-up to a point made by the interviewer can both flatter and impress. Work in something along the lines of, "From what you've mentioned during our conversation, it sounds like your clients are allocating more of their budget to online and interactive. How does this affect the type and quantity of projects that the team will be working on in the near future?"

There are some questions to avoid asking, particularly during a first-round interview. Asking about 401(k)s, salary, or employee benefits may give the impressions that you're more concerned about what you will get from the company than about the work you'll be doing. Although you can ask about the prospects for someone in your position, blatantly asking about how quickly you'll get promoted may make you seem tactless or arrogant. And asking questions about the general state of the industry or the company's plans for the next 10 years may seem vague and canned.

Interview Do's and Don'ts

DON'T

. . . Come unprepared to talk specifically about the company you're interviewing for.
. . . Chew gum or play with your hair.
. . . Dress as if you're headed to either the beach or a nightclub.
. . . Smoke a cigarette beforehand.
. . . Speak badly of anyone, such as a current boss, a teacher, or another company.
. . . Wear heavy perfume, cologne, or makeup.

DO

. . . Research the company beforehand so that you can talk intelligently about its current clients and campaigns.
. . . Come prepared with good questions to ask your interviewer.
. . . Turn off your cell phone (nothing is more embarrassing than hearing your "In Da Club" ring tone in the middle of an interview).
. . . Sit up straight and listen attentively.
. . . Dress more up than down and make sure your clothes are comfortable.
. . . Smile!

After the Interview

You survived the interview and you're out the door. Time to kick back and wait for the offers to roll in, right? Not quite.

Take notes immediately after the interview so you can keep everything straight. Write down your initial impressions of the interviewer, the position, and the workplace. Jot down the main conversation topics, good points you made, and ideas for improving your tactics for interviews in the future. And when you get home, plan out your next steps.

Send a thank-you email to the person (or people) who interviewed you as soon as possible: the same day if you've had a morning inter-

If you interview with multiple people at a particular agency, send each one an individualized thank-you letter, mentioning specific moments from your conversation.

view, and no later than the next morning if you've had a late-afternoon interview. If you're composing a handwritten note, put it in the mail on the same day. Reinforce your interest in the position and reiterate your qualifications. If there were any objections or concerns raised about you as a candidate during your interview, use your thank-you note to respond. For example, you might note that your internship and the extensive reading you've done on your own about the industry overcome your lack of relevant coursework.

SAMPLE THANK-YOU NOTE

Dear Ms. Hiredu,

Thank you for taking the time to talk with me this morning about the assistant media buyer position. DDB Worldwide seems like a unique and engaging place to work, and I am very happy that I got to meet you and see the company firsthand. I enjoyed seeing the media plan for the promotion of the new Anthropologie store. Our talk made me even more excited about an opportunity to work with your team, and I am eager to hear from you.

Sincerely,
Jane Q. Student

642-555-8432
janeq@geemail.com

Unless the company has given you a specific timeline for its decision, you can send a follow-up email after a week. Don't assume that the interviewer remembers everything about you and your conversation. Revisit some of the reasons why you are such a winning candidate. If you discussed something particularly interesting in your interview, you can send a relevant article or your thoughts on an issue to show that you've spent time thinking about it.

Making a Decision

You may hear back immediately, or it may take a company a month or even longer to decide to make an offer. No matter how long it takes, your decision will be expected within a couple of days. The excitement of the offer might tempt you to exercise your *Yes!* impulse, but even if you're sure you want to accept, it's in your best interest to make the decision with care. Consider these factors before committing yourself to spending serious time at a company.

- **What will you be doing all day?** Job descriptions always sound exciting and meaningful, but your typical day won't be loaded with nonstop adventure. How did your interviewer describe the work, and what was the general atmosphere in the office? The most important question to ask yourself is, "Will I be happy going to work each day?"

- **Who's on your team, and how is it structured?** Your coworkers and your boss make all the difference in your work. How did your interviewer describe your team and the office culture? Would you be happy spending 60 hours a week there?

- **What types of client will you be working with?** An agency may have two super-glamorous accounts, but that doesn't mean you'll wind up on one of them. What are their other, less high-profile accounts? Also keep in mind that clients are always switching agencies to get fresh ideas and better bang for their buck, so there's no guarantee who will be there when you arrive. Focus more on a specific agency's mission and overall output than its current client list.

- **Where is it?** Location is key. If your heart is in Kentucky, you might not want to take a job in Los Angeles.

- **How big is it?** In a small company, you'll get to work more closely with all aspects of a campaign, and you might rise to the top quickly (while still doing the filing). But in a large company, there may be more exposure to a wide array of clients and media types. It's up to you to decide what you're looking for.

- **What comes with the deal?** What is the status of the healthcare benefits, 401(k) plans, vacation days, and subsidized gym memberships? Free lunch isn't a make-it-or-break-it part of the deal, but it's certainly a nice perk!

- **Is the salary competitive?** We know that you're not in it for the money, but fair compensation is important. Research the industry standards. Ask human resources about the salary range for the position and be clear about your own expectations, if they ask. If you're switching fields and taking a pay cut, the sacrifice in dollars might be worth the opportunity. And if you're going straight from school, well, money's a novelty, so *any* salary probably sounds great. But it's important that you're satisfied with what you'll be making.

- **How secure is the job?** If the agency suddenly loses the account you'll be working on, will you still have a job? This is a difficult question to ask your prospective employer, but peers or mentors in the industry should be able to give you an honest assessment.

Get all the facts before making your decision. If you're not sure about something, it's perfectly acceptable to follow up with the person offering the job.

66 Don't be proud. Get whatever job you can at an ad agency, then work your way to the job you want to have. If you want to work in advertising, just get a job in the industry. You will soak up all kinds of information by being around the people who are doing what you want to do."

—**Ty Montague,** Chief Creative Officer
JWT

SAYING NO GRACIOUSLY

It's okay to say, "Thanks, but no thanks," if a job offer doesn't sound right. The worst reason to accept a job is out of fear that you won't get another one. If a job doesn't pay fairly, won't challenge you, or simply feels wrong for some other reason, you are totally justified in turning it down.

If you accept an offer immediately and then decide, after further reflection, that you need to turn it down, you risk getting a bad reputation. If you can't avoid going back on your word, talk to your would-be employers in a way that will help them understand your decision. Never burn bridges. Whatever your final answer is, be polite and gracious, and thank your contact for his time and attention. The advertising industry is *really, really* small, and you're almost guaranteed to run into these people again in the future.

7

NAVIGATING YOUR FIRST JOB

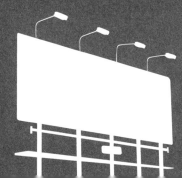

You've arrived at your first job ready to make a splash, get promoted in two weeks, and become best buds with everybody, right? Enthusiasm is great, but navigating the waters of your first job can be tricky. Personalities, politics, and the realization that the stuff you got away with in college won't fly in the real world can be an eye-opener. In this chapter, we'll give you some advice to keep you focused on doing a great job, having fun, and paddling upstream.

BRUSH UP ON WORK BEHAVIOR 101

Were you able to work through those problems with the client? Did you drop the date for getting proofs to the account manager? Did you let that tough art director get under your skin? When you face difficult situations, particularly at the beginning of your career, patience and common sense should guide your behavior. As you move up the professional ladder, your reputation will precede you—so make sure it's spotless.

The Basic Rules

No matter what your position is in the advertising industry, the basic rules of professional behavior apply.

- **Be there.** We don't mean just physically. Every day, be mentally and emotionally present. Don't surf the net all day or chat with friends on IM. Pay attention in meetings, contribute when possible, and be an engaged, active listener. Even if your current role isn't especially challenging or strenuous, there's always a lot to learn. Stay engaged, and you'll better your chances of getting pulled into a new project.

- **Be careful what you type in an email.** Never write anything in an email that you wouldn't mind seeing on the front page of the *New York Times*. Your emails are considered company property and can easily be shared with countless other people or forwarded without your knowledge to a boss, team supervisor, or client. And when you're using your company account, your emails reflect on you as an employee. Keep your messages neat, professional, and to the point. Reread everything before sending, particularly if you're in the midst of a tense situation. Companies regularly monitor their employees' email and Internet activity, so refrain from cursing or writing provocative notes. And whatever you do, never slam one of your coworkers or clients!

- **Volunteer to help.** Roll up your sleeves and pitch in when it comes time to stay late, start a new project, or prepare for a big meeting. Be sure you're not interfering—there may already be a team of people working on it, or a coworker who has been there longer than you may be excited about owning the project. But in general, volunteering to help out on difficult projects will earn you a reputation as a true team player.

66 I was a new AAE with one week under my belt, and a more senior AAE needed help proofreading. I volunteered to help out, and it turned out to be a much bigger project than they had anticipated. I stayed until well past 1 A.M. editing, proofreading, and spell-checking. It was a killer, but it got the word out that I was a team player willing to pitch in and stay late."

—**Allison Schwarz,** Brand Manager
Citigroup

- **Tidy up.** Make sure your desk is clean when you leave every day. Not only does tidying up keep you organized, but it also shows that you respect your job, your workplace, and your coworkers. If someone needs to check in on one of your projects while you're out of the office, they'll appreciate how easily they can find the materials they need. Plus it just feels good to arrive each morning to a neat workplace.

- **Keep your personal life personal.** Especially during the first couple of months, it's important to keep your personal life separate from your work life. No matter how nice or interested they seem, your coworkers don't need to know about your pot-smoking roommate or messy on-again, off-again hook-up fest with your ex. After you've developed solid friendships, you can talk about your other interests over drinks after work. But in the office, keep your personal details to yourself.

- **Be friendly.** A smile goes a long way, as do "hello," "please," and "thank you."

***

Instant reputation

In many companies, people communicate via IM. It's a quick, easy way to stay in touch with members of your team or other departments. If you're working at a firm that uses IM, make sure your screen name is professional. Trade in "soccerdiva23" for something appropriate for the office. And don't slip into the habit of chatting with friends all day. There's nothing worse than sitting at your desk with your boss when "What a crazy night!" pops up on the screen.

***

10 Ways to Make Your Boss Rue the Day He Hired You

1. **Don't dress the part.** Even as an intern (*especially* as an intern, actually), don't dress below company standards. And if you have even the slightest inkling that your boss may ask you to see a client, don't show up in a wrinkled shirt.

2. **Turn up your nose at the little tasks.** If you cop an attitude when you're asked to do basic tasks like photocopying or filing, you'll get a reputation as a brat. Everyone's had to pay dues, so no one will sympathize with your airs of superiority.

3. **Gossip.** Don't talk about anyone in the office—especially your boss. Even if everyone else is doing it, as your mother might remind you, that doesn't make it right. No need to be holier-than-thou when other people gossip, but keep your own nose clean.

4. **Date anyone in the office.** You're surrounded by new people and you're suddenly spending more time with them than you are with your friends. Intense feelings can develop, and it's natural to find yourself crushing on a coworker. But that's where it should end. Inter-office dating, especially early on in your career, will make life difficult. This is doubly true if the crush in question is your superior.

5. **Don't work a full day.** Your job description says you work nine to five, but that doesn't mean you get to leave at 5 P.M. on the dot. When you're first at an agency, nothing can affect your rep more than the hours you work. If your coworkers stay late, make sure you're right there with them.

6. **Bring your personal life into the workplace.** Don't spend half your day making personal calls on your cell phone. Keep your own business to a minimum and stay focused on learning the ins and outs of project planning and client service.

7. **Go over your boss's head.** If you want to alienate your new boss fast, try going behind his back and getting buddy-buddy with *his* boss. If you have a question or concern, or if you need someone to look over your creative brief, go to your immediate supervisor first.

8. **Record every detail of your job on the web.** You probably signed an NDA (nondisclosure agreement) when you began your job, and that agreement covers the Internet. Do not start a blog detailing life at a top-10 ad agency or reveal confidential information about your clients, product launches, or ad campaigns.

9. **Take it to Web 2.0.** When you're the new kid in the office, your coworkers will be wary of you. Don't test the limits of their trust by taking office videos or photos of your client's products and posting them on your MySpace account without permission.

10. **Cry.** Never cry in view of any coworker. Ever.

MANAGE YOUR OFFICE RELATIONSHIPS

A huge part of office life is getting along with others. This goes beyond the teamwork and leadership qualities listed on your résumé. You'll need to know how to collaborate with your colleagues to get anything done. But you'll also need to adapt to people's styles and stay out of the fray of messy office politics if you're going to survive. Your relationship with your boss and other high-ranking superiors will be different from that with coworkers and team members, and navigating this terrain can be tricky. Here's a map.

Your and Your Boss

At your first job, your primary objective will be helping your boss with whatever she needs so she looks as good as possible to her boss and clients. Whether you're sending a mock-up to a client, preparing the status reports for a team meeting, or updating the creative binder, do what you can to ensure that things run smoothly. Proving that you can handle small tasks is a giant step toward acquiring new responsibilities and greater autonomy.

Spend time observing your boss's behavior. You'll learn how often she comes in early, works late, eats at her desk, and takes vacations. You'll see how often she speaks with clients and other departments and if she does so via phone, email, or face-to-face. You'll listen to the tone of voice she uses with colleagues and notice the writing style she employs in official emails. You'll learn a lot from watching and working with her, and she can be an invaluable source of advice and support as you grow and advance.

Once you've worked with the same supervisor for a few months, you'll probably be able to anticipate what she wants and how she wants it done. To get to that point, keep these tips in mind.

- **Get to know your boss's communication style.** Every boss communicates with employees a little differently. Some like all client communications documented in email. Some like every meeting scheduled and get flustered if you pop into their office unannounced. Others will feel anxious if you're not constantly coming by to provide updates. Observe how your boss works and adapt your communication style accordingly.

- **Ask questions.** The advertising industry is extremely fast paced and often hectic. Mistakes can be costly, so even if things are crazy, go to your boss if you need help. If you don't understand exactly what's being asked of you, clarify. Your boss will be more upset if you stay quiet and make a wrong decision than if you interrupt his busy day to ask a question. To save time, be specific, as in, "Where do we store competitive materials from past years?"

BlackBerry etiquette

BlackBerrys used to be status symbols in advertising agencies, the mark of a supervisor or above. These days, it's common for entry-level employees to get BlackBerrys so their supervisors can reach them all the time. First-time users *beware:* BlackBerrys are highly addictive; hence the "CrackBerry" nickname. Here's how to avoid the faux pas that first-time users often make.

- Don't use your BlackBerry during a face-to-face conversation with someone.

- Don't use your BlackBerry and drive a car at the same time.

- During meetings, put your BlackBerry away or facedown on the table to show your undivided attention.

- If you're expecting an important email, set the device to vibrate and alert the people you're with that you might need to take a moment.

- Don't email people at all hours of the night or over the weekend and expect an immediate response. Likewise, if someone emails you at one of those times, you're not necessarily obligated to respond right away. Some things really can wait.

- Don't get lazy and allow yourself to make typos just because the keyboard is a little harder to use.

- **Double-check your work.** Anything you send out, whether it's to a client or another department, reflects on you, your boss, your team, and your agency. Mathematical mistakes, typos, or simple grammatical errors look unprofessional and dim-witted. Your boss isn't your teacher. She won't have the patience or the time to review your work and give you endless opportunities for revision. When you submit a report or project, always edit your work carefully for mistakes. And remember, presentation counts! Make sure that everything you give to your boss—competitive analyses, reports, conceptual printouts, sample materials, and so on—is orderly and error free.

> 66 I was taught in school that the last item in a list should be preceded by a comma. When I began my first job as an assistant account executive, I noticed that my boss and other members of the team didn't do that, so I began inserting the missing commas. Bad idea. My boss pulled me aside and explained that in advertising, you leave out the comma before the last item. She said I really ought to observe before assuming that everyone around me lacked grammar skills."

> —**Randi Zuckerberg,** Marketing Director
> Facebook

- **Never correct your boss during a meeting.** Even when your boss is wrong, don't embarrass him in front of his colleagues and employees. If it's an important mistake, stop by his office or send a polite email afterward. Briefly explain why you think he made an error: "The numbers you presented in the meeting were accurate for last week, but I was just checking the spreadsheet and noticed that this week's numbers are a little different." Or soften your comment by phrasing it as a question: "Were we going to use the blond twins on the bicycles or the brunette twins with the hula hoops?"

- **Provide some status.** Some bosses love it if you walk into their office every day with a status update on your projects together, rattling off the details of every meeting and deliverable so that they can focus on other things. Consistent status reports can keep your boss in the loop and make her feel confident that you have everything under control. However, not all bosses appreciate constant barrages of information, so observe and act accordingly.

- **Request deadlines.** In an entry-level position, you may have multiple people giving you assignments. Ask everyone to give you a deadline, no matter how small the project. Something that seems low priority could be needed at the printer's the next day. If you ask for clarification, you'll be able to organize your workload more effectively and keep people from showing up at your desk, demanding the project they gave you yesterday.

- **Make your boss look good whenever possible.** Your boss has a boss too, and she wants to look good for her supervisors just as much as you do. If your boss has a meeting, make sure all the materials are ready and waiting for her. Don't wait until three minutes before to start photocopying. If it's a *really* important meeting, stay by your phone in case she needs anything. This would be the wrong time to say, "Nice! She's gone for an hour. Let's go get coffee!"

- **Remember your place.** Although it's okay to speak up in meetings, always defer to your boss. Run ideas by him before you present them to the group. Don't invite trouble by going over his head with an idea or promising something to a client without telling him first. A boss who distrusts or resents you can single-handedly make work a miserable place.

- **When you don't know something, admit it.** If you have enough information to make an educated guess, do so; but if you don't have a clue, don't fake it. Lying or fudging the details will make you appear untrustworthy in the eyes of your supervisor and coworkers. Usually a simple, "I don't know," will do. Whenever you can, follow up that admission with a specific offer, such as, "I can find out by this afternoon," or, "I expect the mocks to be here by Tuesday."

- **Don't be afraid to say something if you're really overwhelmed.** If you've been given 15 high-priority assignments and you know you can't possibly get to all of them, don't just silently stress. You'll anger people by completing projects shoddily or failing to complete them at all. Talk to your boss, explain the situation, and ask her to help you prioritize. This will make you look proactive and organized and will give you the chance to move some projects around.

CROSSING THE GENERATION GAP

The current generation of entry-level job seekers (sometimes referred to as *millennials*) shares some distinctive expectations about the workplace and their careers. Millennials feel entitled to speak their minds freely and anticipate that their opinions will be heard and valued. They expect immediate gratification and want to progress rapidly without wasting their time on tasks they consider beneath them.

We get it. You want to have your voice heard, you want your opinions to be respected, and you don't want to spend your day making photocopies. But the older generation—the Gen X-ers and baby boomers who constitute your bosses and coworkers—may view you as arrogant and entitled. Don't live up to those negative expectations. Prove them wrong by being an incredible team player with an eager, can-do attitude.

If you feel that your boss is out of touch, join the club. But even if your boss thinks Firefox is a new breed of dog and can't keep up with the latest developments in wikis, podcasts, and user-generated content, he still has a great deal to teach you. When working with older colleagues, consider how much they know. They have an invaluable background in traditional advertising and precious knowledge about how the industry has changed. These people have spent years establishing themselves in this industry. They deserve respect, so make a point of asking their opinion and really listening when they give it. Even if you are truly exceptional, you need to respect structure and seniority. A little deference will get you a long way.

WHEN YOUR BOSS IS OLD ENOUGH TO BE YOUR . . . SISTER?

Advertising agencies attract a younger crowd at some positions, and you might end up with a boss who's very close to you in age. The good news: You may find it easier to communicate with a younger boss, and you'll probably have more in common with him than you would with someone significantly older. The challenge: It's easy to see your boss as a friend and forget to treat him like a supervisor or to think you can get away with more because you had the same lunchbox growing up.

Despite his stature, a young boss may need to grow into his role, both emotionally and professionally. He may feel threatened by you or see you as a competitor rather than someone who can help. He may feel the need to assert his authority by exerting more control over you than is necessary. Or he may be the one who treats the relationship a little too familiarly. He may talk a bit too much and draw you into situations where you're gossiping about others. Either way, it wouldn't hurt to be cautious and remind yourself to treat him as you would any superior.

KEEPING IT PROFESSIONAL

No matter how old your boss is, she is in charge, and your behavior should reflect her authority. Don't spend too much time chatting about your personal life. If your boss knows that you're consumed with grief over your breakup, she might assume that you won't do a good job on your projects. That new guy you've been dating, the unemployed sister in town, your parents' divorce—save those for happy hour with your friends, and keep your work conversations professional.

That goes double for serious topics such as mental health or substance abuse. Don't assume that private confessions will stay private. Your boss has an obligation to follow human resources guidelines if you reveal shocking information about yourself, which might include disclosure of information.

Legal matters

If you're asked to do something illegal or immoral, don't feel bad about quitting, even if you've been with the company for only a brief time. Here's a list of things employers shouldn't ask you to do.

- Work without filing taxes or reporting your income. Not only is working under the table illegal, but it also hurts you in the long run, because you won't be contributing to your own Social Security account.

- Misrepresent the company or its products.

- See you socially, one-on-one (as in a date, for example).

- Spend your own money on company business without reimbursement.

Your boss may be the one sharing personal details about his life, which puts you in an awkward position. You don't want to appear uninterested in his life, but you want to establish an appropriately professional relationship. Don't get drawn into gossip or offer advice on his personal life. If he is going on and on about, say, his sex life, just smile or nod politely and chuckle when prompted. Don't respond with a personal story of your own. Just keep your hands on your keyboard or your eyes on your mock-ups, and he'll get the hint that you'd like to get back to your work.

Staff Hierarchies and Office Politics

Whether you're working at a 10-person creative boutique or a publicly traded holding company, you'll be walking into a group dynamic that already exists. Pay attention to these cues for finding your place.

- **Listen and learn from everyone.** If an assistant account executive who's been there a year longer than you suggests that you do something a certain way, don't dismiss her because she's not a manager. Respect her seniority and recognize that you can learn from her experience.

- **Stay away from drama.** People *love* drama, and they love to complain about their coworkers. If you have a tendency to gossip, do your best to stay neutral. You can empathize with someone's bad day without taking sides. And although it's tempting to share a juicy story, it's also the quickest way to alienate yourself. A reputation for indiscretion can hurt your chances for promotion down the road.

- **Don't expect everything to be fair.** You might think that everyone always seems to get more recognition than you. Even if your indignation is warranted, don't focus on the injustice of the situation. Focus on doing your job well and contributing to the group. If you don't think your work is being properly acknowledged, find a professional way to keep your boss updated, like emphasizing your successes in your weekly status meeting or team staff meetings.

- **Earn a rep as a team player.** A great attitude will take you a long way. When you finish your work, tell your boss that you're ready for more. If you seek out tasks and do even the grunt work cheerfully, you'll be thought of as a hardworking, enthusiastic team player, and you'll be rewarded when the time comes.

- **Check your ego at the door.** Now that you're a full-fledged member of the workforce, guess what? No one cares what you did before you joined the company. And as beautiful as your Harvard diploma is, it won't do your work for you. People want to know if you're good at your job and if you can get things done. They don't want to know about your past life as a superstar.

- **Keep your blog to yourself.** It seems like everyone's got a blog these days. Privacy? *Pshaw!* That kind of attitude is all well and good among your friends, but when you have a job, your blog can get you in a lot of trouble. Remember that NDA? Posting any info about your job, clients, or workplace—no matter how trivial or seemingly anonymous— directly violates that agreement and could result in your termination. Not to mention the lack of trust you'll engender if coworkers get wind of your blogging escapades.

Researching your promotion

Knowing how long most people in your position waited before getting a promotion can help you gauge your progress and save you a lot of grief. If the typical assistant holds a position for one-and-a-half to two years before getting promoted, you shouldn't take it as a personal attack if you get overlooked after your first. On the other hand, you should make it known that you're interested in doing what it takes to move up.

Mixing Business with Pleasure

You'll spend most of your waking hours at work. Naturally, you'll form friendships with the people slaving away beside you. It's easy—and smart—to bond with that account manager or copywriter over a few beers. Work friends can be wonderful sources of support and encouragement, because they understand exactly what you're going through. But work relationships occupy a special place in the friendship realm and should be treated accordingly. When you're all on the same payroll—and potentially jockeying for the same promotions and the same high-profile projects—things can get sticky.

SOCIALIZING WITH COWORKERS

Advertising is a party-happy industry, and agency folk have the tendency to let their hair down more than people in other industries. Watch your step: This can be as dangerous as it is fun. The feelings of intimacy you develop with coworkers can get deceptively comfortable. Comfort will lead to indiscreet confessions and gossip, and this will lead to a reputation as exclusive or snobby, or worse. Make an effort to be outgoing with everyone, especially those in other departments. Not only does this make for a more pleasant workplace, it also paves the way for a small favor or two down the road.

One major caution: Don't get so liquored up at company happy hour that you spill your guts about your deep dislike of the creative director or let everyone know that you caught two coworkers canoodling in the media library. Pole dancing while wearing a Santa cap or doing body shots off your cubicle-mate might seem incredibly funny and appropriate at the time, but will you still think so the next day? Don't get trashed, don't gossip, and don't say or do anything you'll regret. Otherwise, guess what the choice gossip will be at the next event?

66 Please, keep your wits about you at events. As much fun as an open bar is, it's not as much fun as everybody else will have talking about you the next day! To wit, Poopy Pants, who in her first week of working at an agency got so drunk at the Fox Upfront that she . . . well, the nickname pretty much says it all. She had to be removed from the party and was, not surprisingly, fired the next day. This did not prevent the story from spreading like wildfire, eventually making its way to the *New York Post*! This is single-handedly the most oft-told cautionary tale to any new employee."

—**Erica Slomak,** National Broadcast Negotiator
MindShare

> Don't flaunt your close friendships by making weekend plans, going out for coffee midday, or inviting only select people for the post-work drink or three.

DATING AT WORK

Dating at work is rarely a good idea. It's very easy for other employees to gossip about the details, and nowhere do issues of competition or advancement get more complicated. That's not to mention the disaster that could ensue if you break up or if one of you becomes the other's boss.

If you really do develop a strong relationship with a coworker, exercise caution, take things slow, and keep it as quiet as possible. Don't reveal details to others (even if you trust someone; the other person in your relationship may not), and refrain from spending unnecessary time together during the workday. What you do on your own time is your business. But while you're at work, your relationship is like a flashing billboard in Times Square, and your gossipy coworkers can't wait to tell everyone what it says.

10 Things to Avoid at the Company Holiday Party

1. **Talking only to people from your small team.** Company parties provide a fabulous networking opportunity. You have the chance to chat with people in the other departments or senior employees you wouldn't normally spend time around.

2. **Hooking up with anyone.** No matter how good an idea it seems at the time, don't engage in any office party romancing—especially with a superior.

3. **Saying anything bad about your coworkers or company.** You never know when the charming young thing you're chatting up will turn out to be the boss's kid.

4. **Getting trashed.** Don't drink so much that you end the night slumped on the bathroom floor.

5. **Wearing too little.** Don't dress in something too small, too tight, too short, or too transparent.

6. **Dancing provocatively** . . . or badly.

7. **Partaking of "party favors."** Don't slip outside for a little extra fun in the form of recreational drugs.

8. **Hanging on your date like cling wrap.** Especially if that date is a coworker.

9. **Stealing anything.** Wine, centerpieces, utensils . . . you name it—don't take it.

10. **Bringing work for your boss to look at.** There's a time and a place for work, and office parties aren't it.

Don't create gossip. Consider a holiday party a success if no one remembers anything about your role in it—other than your effervescent wit and sparkling charm, of course.

TAKE CRITICISM GRACEFULLY

Criticism is part of any job. Even if you manage to avoid major screwups, there will come a time when your work, behavior, or style rubs someone the wrong way. Keep it all in perspective. Nobody's perfect, and hearing that you need to improve doesn't mean that you're inept or getting fired.

When your boss sits you down and tells you that you made a mistake, don't cry, get huffy, or list all the great things you've done that he doesn't appreciate. Be open to the feedback. Treat it as a learning experience. Listen carefully, get specific examples, and ask for guidance on how to fix the problem. If you get to the end of the conversation and you still don't understand what you need to do differently, ask. Neither you nor your boss wants to have this conversation again.

Dealing with Reviews

A review is not a personal attack but an opportunity to improve yourself and your job skills. Whatever the critique is, ask your boss for specific instances of your missteps, and work with her to outline some specific steps of improvement. We all want to hear that we're doing a fabulous job, but that usually doesn't happen. And even if your performance is 99 percent fabulous, your boss can still probably tell you about a few areas where you could improve. Otherwise, you'd be her boss! So if you get a review that's less than stellar, don't get mad—get better.

Reviews in advertising remain fairly standard across departments and agencies, so after you survive your first one, you'll know what to expect in the future. Here are some tips on keeping your cool (and your perspective) during your review.

- **Note the "growth areas."** Know this going in: Your boss *has* to name an area where you can improve. If your boss sat you down, told you that you're awesome, and patted you on the back, the process would be totally pointless, and you would know nothing new about how you can grow professionally. Even if you're a star, your boss will discuss some element of your performance that could be improved on.

- **Listen and learn, but don't obsess.** Don't take criticism personally, and don't focus on the negative aspects of your review. So your boss thinks you need to do a better job of keeping people in the loop. That's not so bad. He didn't tell you that you're hopeless and incompetent. He's just giving you advice that, if you follow it, will help you be more respected by your peers. Keep it all in perspective.

- **If you get a harsh critique, resolve to make a real change.** If you get a harsher-than-expected warning, pay attention. Before you leave the review, make sure you understand what's expected of you and what behavioral changes your boss wants (or needs) to see. If she requests a big change, discuss steps you can take to demonstrate improvement. Then take those steps. If you've been reprimanded for leaving early when everyone else is staying late and slaving away, adjust your schedule so that you can stay longer at the office, and keep two nights a week free so that you will be available to work late if necessary. On the other hand, don't overreact and sleep at the office every night for the next two weeks.

- **Focus on yourself.** The only thing going on when you're in that room is your own review. Don't use this as an opportunity to bash a coworker, even if you have a strong opinion about her performance or feel that her poor work ethic has made it difficult for you to get your job done.

> **It is your fault**
>
> In advertising, you're going to be in the position of depending on other people. If someone doesn't get you materials in time and you're late turning something in to your boss, guess what? You're responsible for your end of the project. Do what you can to stay on top of things, and if you know something's going to get to you late, update your boss. They're less likely to be irritated if they know ahead of time. You'll earn more respect from your superiors through your honesty and hard work than you will by making excuses, blaming other people, or getting upset.

- **Don't flip out.** If the feedback you receive is truly off base, you can always respond by sending a brief, written response to human resources and your boss. It's okay to share your side of the story with specific examples of your contributions and accomplishments. However, don't fight back during the review. Cool off for a couple of days. Write your response when you're calm and have taken the time to back up your position with detailed examples.

- **Do not cry.** If you find yourself getting emotional or losing your cool, do whatever it takes to calm down. Bite your tongue, grit your teeth, anything. Just don't cry, and don't get angry. If you're on the brink of breaking down in front of your boss, excuse yourself to go to the restroom or get some water. Don't let her add "unstable" to the list of your shortcomings.

- **And if you're on the chopping block . . .** If your boss tells you that you're on probation and could be fired, take it seriously and look into your company's termination policy. Employers are generally required to give you a written statement outlining the reasons for your probation, along with requests for improvement and a time frame within which you need to accomplish the requested changes. Usually, an employee is given 90 days to improve before she can be fired. Your human resources department will be helpful in figuring out these details.

Reviews can be positive and encouraging. They can also be nerve-racking. If you're a creative, it's difficult to separate yourself emotionally from the work you've done. If you're in account management, it's hard to hear that a client had a negative comment about your work. If you're in media, it's painful to find out that all your work paid off in a poor ROI. But life goes on. A comment about your work isn't a comment about you personally. Keeping work in perspective will help you go far in this industry.

Preparing for your annual review

Before your official review, you may be asked to write a self-evaluation. What have you done well? What could you improve? What are your goals? Even if you're not asked to do it, it can be a good way to prepare yourself for what's to come. Chances are that your self-penned review will closely resemble your boss's. Analyzing yourself will prepare you to accept criticism and allow you to pinpoint major discrepancies between your view of your work and your boss's view. Your preparedness will come out in the review, and your supervisor will appreciate that you take the process seriously.

Walk into the meeting with solid evidence of your performance and info on your key achievements of the year. Be prepared to speak about your professional goals for the following year. Do you want to manage a project on your own? Learn how to write a creative brief? Run an offsite photo shoot? Part of the review process is demonstrating your continuing interest in and enthusiastic for your job.

Oh, and be on time.

TURNING DOWN A PROMOTION

You're talented, creative, and all-around wonderful. Your boss recognizes this and proposes a change in your position. This change might be a wonderful opportunity, or it might be an ill-advised move. Turning down a promotion can be tough, but sometimes it's the right step. Here are a few circumstances that might make a promotion less than desirable.

- **The new job requires you to relocate, but you have obligations in your current location.** Maybe you have an aging parent or significant other you'd like to be near. Perhaps you've just invested in property.

- **The new job involves significantly different working conditions.** Maybe you've been working full-time in the office and your new position would require a great deal of travel. That might be exciting the first few times, but could you do it for 30 weeks straight? If a big lifestyle change is involved, ask yourself whether you would enjoy it.

- **The new job would entail a significantly different role.** The promotion might be an amazing opportunity, but if you have a clear goal of where you want to be in the future and this new job takes you away from that, you may want to reconsider. If you take the promotion, you'll have to stay *at least* a year or two, and that long detour from your desired career path might derail you.

If you do turn down a promotion or transfer, make sure the company knows how honored you were to be considered and how happy you are with your current situation. If you've thought this out and decided that it's really not right for you, they'll respect your wishes. But if you're indelicate or vague, you could risk offending someone or, worse yet, leave them with the impression that you're just not into more work and responsibility.

WHEN YOU'RE DUE FOR A REVIEW AND NOBODY GIVES YOU ONE

Most agencies have a formal review process that is run, or at least monitored, by the human resources department. However, sometimes the HR department falls behind schedule or an agency conducts their reviews informally. You might find yourself six months or a year into a job with no sign of formal feedback. Your first reaction might be to breathe a sigh of relief, but you should also keep in mind that a review is a great opportunity to receive comments on your work, improve your skills, and plot your course for the coming months. You're entitled to a yearly review, and you deserve one. If it appears that you've been overlooked, it's okay to ask your boss or HR to set one up.

LEARN ON THE JOB

Luckily for you, you can learn most of what you need to know on the job. Many people enter advertising right after college, and a high percentage of those entry-level workers have never worked full-time in the industry before.

66 Nothing you do as a media buyer will be remotely close to anything you learned in school or did at a previous job. Basically you are learning a new language, completely new software, and new math. It takes three months to get comfortable and six months to really have a handle on what you are doing and talking about. Just stick with it and ask *lots and lots* of questions."

—**Erica Slomak,** National Broadcast Negotiator
MindShare

Seeking a Mentor

You wouldn't run a marathon without talking to some experienced runners, would you? Likewise, you don't want to jump into advertising without a veteran to show you the ropes.

Mentors can be a great influence on your work and your life. A seasoned professional can answer your questions and provide perspective. She can tell you where advertising has been and where it's going. She can help you with everything from getting insider info to navigating tricky office politics to educating you about what the future might hold as you move up in the company.

Some larger companies have formal mentor programs. If it's optional, sign up. If you haven't heard about it, speak to someone in your human resources department to see if your agency has one. Your mentor will likely be someone from a close group, not your own, who will meet with you on a regular basis, give you feedback on your daring new ideas, and answer the questions you might not feel comfortable asking anyone else.

If you're not getting enough feedback from your boss or certain aspects of work mystify you, look around for someone else to learn from informally. It might be a senior employee from another department who you connect with, a fellow alum from your alma mater, or an old supervisor or client. If you can identify someone whom you respect and who gives off a friendly vibe, take the first step by sending an email inviting him to grab coffee.

Learning from Your Colleagues

You can learn a lot from your colleagues. Strike up a conversation in the elevator or ask about a photo on someone's desk. You'd be amazed what can come from asking, "Is that a picture of your beagle wearing a bunny costume?" Once you're friendly with your coworkers, you can ask them questions and get their advice.

You can also learn a great deal from colleagues outside your company. Get involved with professional organizations such as the AAAA or local industry groups tailored to young professionals in your city. Attend advertising networking events and career development panels. Arrange for coffee in the morning or drinks after work with people you meet. It takes more than a "hello" to turn a potential contact into a professional friend, so get out there and make an effort.

Adgoraphobia

Navigating events can be awkward even for the most social of us. Here are some ways to make a room full of strangers less scary.

- For the first couple of events, arrive close to the beginning so that you can warm up with a more manageable crowd. Say hello to the people sitting next to you and try to get a few business cards.

- Look for people you know from previous events. Say hello and introduce yourself to the people they're talking to.

- Find people who work for a company you know and introduce yourself. You can simply say, "Hi, you work for McCann Erikson? I'm Naomi Glen. I work on the Nike campaign at Avenue A." If nothing else, follow that up with a remark about the event.

Staying Sharp

Just because you have a job doesn't mean you can turn off your brain. You will be learning throughout your career, and all of those resources you consulted while looking for a job can help build your industry knowledge and keep your skills up-to-date once you've got one. Staying informed will help you do your job and will keep you competitive in the job market. Here are a few tips.

- **Read everything you can get your hands on.** Many companies subscribe to major advertising industry magazines. Read these during your lunch break or check them out on your commute home. There will only be a few copies of each issue floating around the office, and if you're pretty low on the food chain, you may have to wait a few weeks to get your hands on one. Consider subscribing to a few of these magazines on your own, and keep up with industry websites.

- **Utilize your company's educational opportunities.** Many agencies run onsite workshops on a range of topics and skills. Other companies provide assistance to pay for continuing education classes. Going to seminars and enrolling in training programs will keep your skills up-to-date and give you a great opportunity to meet other people in your company.

- **Get connected to the industry.** Join an advertising trade organization or attend local industry events. Take notes and ask questions.

THINK AHEAD

Barring outlandish success or cataclysmic failure, your first job won't be your last. In fact, the average 20-something can expect to have as many as five different *careers* before he retires. There's always that one guy who's been with the company for 50 years and gets recognized at the office holiday party, but the majority of people bounce around faster than name cards can be created for their cubicles.

No matter how much you love your job and hate to think of leaving, you should always have the next step in mind and be ready to take an amazing opportunity if it falls into your lap. Seek the advice of your mentor, assuming she isn't your direct boss. Even after you've changed companies or departments, keep in touch with the people you used to work with. As they progress in their careers and advance to positions of power elsewhere, they'll be valuable contacts and sources of information—not to mention terrific recommendations when you next apply.

Planning Your Next Move

Plan on staying at your first job for at least a year or two. Anything less than that and you risk burning a bridge. Agencies spend six to 12 months getting a new employee up to speed, and they won't be happy if you up and leave just as your training period is ending.

You may adore your job right now, but at some point you'll probably get itchy and think seriously about leaving and exploring another opportunity. It's important to make sure you're leaving for the right reasons. Before you dive head-on into another job search, ask yourself the following questions.

- **Have I learned everything I can from this job?** A wise mentor once said, "As long as you're learning more than you're giving, it's worth it to stay. It's when you stop learning that you're ready to leave."

- **Have I been in this job for at least a year?** If you haven't stayed at least a full year, potential employers might see you as flaky.

- **Is this a lateral move?** A lateral move is a like-titled job at a similar company. An upward move—which is far more desirable—can be a promotion within your current company, a more prestigious position at a similar firm, or a similar position at a more prestigious firm. If you're thinking of making a lateral move, consider the fact that you may have to start over again, getting used to a new company's politics and procedures and building a new degree of seniority. However, if you're currently working in account management and decide that your real calling lies in media, you may just have to suck it up and become an assistant somewhere new.

- **What am I getting myself into?** Scope out the other job. Do the people get along with each other? If you're replacing someone, why did she leave? Here's where your network comes in. Ask your contacts if they know anyone at this new company, and then call up your new second-degree friends to tactfully get the inside scoop.

- **Am I leaving for the right reasons?** When you start a job, you can't predict what will happen in your life down the road. It makes sense to leave an agency in New York City because your fiancé just accepted a terrific offer in San Francisco or because your family's business needs your help. Your current boss and coworkers are likely to understand and be supportive if you have sensible reasons for leaving. However, if you're leaving because of the long hours, you made a mistake and someone got mad at you, or your boss is mean, you're running *from* the job. Instead of jumping ship, identify steps you can take to resolve the problem or places you can move within your own company.

- **Is it a personality issue?** Even though you are the model of professionalism, there might be people at your job you just can't stand to work with. If you've tried *everything*—being nice, asking for their advice, offering to help with one of their projects—it might be time to talk with your supervisor about switching departments or teams. If the problem is with your boss, don't blab to everyone that you're not getting along, but do seek wise counsel from a mentor outside of your team or agency.

- **How does this move fit into my long-term career plan?** Switching jobs should improve your life in at least one of these three areas: what you do all day, where you do it, or who you do it with. Don't move to a new job just to make a few extra thousand dollars a year. If the new job is a great opportunity that will open up more doors for you, go for it. If you don't have a clear sense of where the job might lead, consider staying put a bit longer and gaining more experience.

8

EXPLORING RELATED OPPORTUNITIES

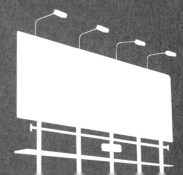

A dvertising is a big, exciting, and diverse world—but it's just the tip of the communications iceberg. There are tons of jobs that all aim, as advertising does, to get the word out. Below is an overview of some key roles in the marketing and publishing industries that will also help you exercise your creative, analytical, and social muscles.

MARKETING

Marketing is everywhere. From subway ads for the new iPod, to American Express's sponsorship of the U.S. Open, to exclusive events promoting Johnnie Walker Red, anytime a company sends out a message, you're experiencing the effects of its marketing effort.

According to the marketing reference site knowthis.com, over 30 percent of all jobs globally fall under the marketing category.

Because marketing and advertising are so closely related, they're often confused with each other. But advertising is just one component of a company's **marketing communications mix:** the combination of advertising, sales, public relations, and marketing used to support a company's revenue goals. Before an ad agency can create a campaign that conveys a strong message about a brand's identity, someone must first develop and articulate what that brand identity is. And after the ad agency collects its paycheck and heads home, someone must make sure that the message continues to be conveyed consistently. All of these activities fall under the broad banner of marketing.

The marketing department is responsible for defining the target audience and managing the company's relationship with it. These people figure out what the target audience wants, from product features to services to price, and help develop the product and message accordingly. To accomplish this goal, companies develop strategies in interactive marketing, trade marketing, market research, direct marketing, and brand marketing.

The eMarketing Association (emarketing association.com), is a great source for news, events, contacts, and, most importantly, job listings.

- **Interactive marketing:** Interactive marketers manage the online relationship between the buyer and the seller by advising on and implementing the best uses for social networks, blogs, chatbots, and wikis. Once a small niche, it's now one of the most important areas in the field. Many large ad agencies have departments that specialize in interactive marketing, while some firms handle only interactive marketing and nothing else. Because young people make up the core consumers of emerging media, entry-level 20-somethings are valued for their opinions and expertise on youth culture. As a result, this is becoming a hot area for recent grads. Working in interactive marketing doesn't require much knowledge of HTML or Java—a separate web development group usually handles the programming end. But you'll be expected to stay up-to-date on trends and new developments online.

Interactive marketing firms

As the Internet's influence becomes ever more pervasive, there has been a jump in the number of companies that specialize in, or devote themselves exclusively to, online marketing. Here are some of the top dogs.

EVB (evb.com)**:** This San Fran–based specialist in experimental marketing handles accounts for Wrigley's, Burger King, and Adidas, to name a few. Their recent "MLS Mashup" website combines music, video, and soccer to promote Adidas's involvement in the 2006 MLS play-offs. EVB was recently acquired by Omnicom.

Advertising.com: Opening a couple of years before the dotcom bust, Advertising.com has led the way in online ad placement and tracking. Now a major player in the online marketing world, Advertising.com made big news when it became a subsidiary of AOL in 2004.

DoubleClick (doubleclick.com)**:** A major provider of online ads and research tools, DoubleClick helps direct marketers and advertisers analyze and optimize their online marketing efforts. Started in 1996, the infancy of online marketing, DoubleClick now has offices across the United States, Europe, Asia, and Australia.

Spacedog (spacedoghouse.com)**:** One look at the space age website tells you all you need to know about this hip California-based agency characterized by youth-oriented, YouTube-influenced campaigns. Clients include Qantas, Hitachi, Warner Brothers, and Carl's, Jr's. Charbroiled Burgers, for whose website they earned an Internet Advertising Award in 2006.

- **Trade marketing:** Trade marketers create informational and promotional materials for the company's executive and sales teams. Audiovisual presentations, brochures, sales samples, and tchotchkes all come from trade marketing. Starting out in this area involves perfecting PowerPoint presentations, finagling spreadsheets, and polishing documents. This may sound tedious, but the work will put you in direct contact with other departments and give you tremendous insight into everything going on inside the company. Also, since most of the work you do is intended for company supervisors and executives, you'll have visibility among some of the top brass, providing an excellent opportunity for prime networking.

- **Market research:** Market researchers gather data about potential consumers. They ask: Who is buying this type of product? How do these people spend their time online? What other products do they buy? Where are the new markets to target, and how can we reach them? They then analyze the answers to make decisions about product development and marketing. As a market analyst, you may run focus groups, work with subscription services such as Nielsen, comScore, and @plan to get target market data, and compile information in spreadsheets to share with other departments in your company. It's a hands-on field that involves a direct connection to media outlets. Successful market researchers love compiling and analyzing numbers and data and tend to be detail oriented, organized, and articulate.

The Direct Marketing Association (the-dma.org) is a global trade organization for direct marketing. It has a handy job bank for those looking for work!

- **Direct marketing:** While ads are intended for mass consumption, direct marketing campaigns target a narrower audience. Direct marketers create personal, often interactive materials in the hopes of appealing to a specific consumer. They send all those catalogs to your mailbox, produce infomercials on DirectTV or satellite radio, and send the emails you receive after joining a group or signing up for a subscription. Because of advances in communication technology, particularly the Internet, companies can now track the habits and desires of potential customers in a cheap, accurate way, and then communicate directly with these consumers. This field has grown recently as a result. Increasingly, direct marketing is not just a supplement to other promotional efforts, but the main, or sometimes only, marketing tool that a company employs.

Not your grandma's direct-mail catalog

In the old days, people associated direct marketing with junk mail and telemarketers who called in the middle of dinner. Well, those techniques are still widely used. In 2005, for example, more than 114 billion pieces of direct mail were sent to mailboxes in the United States. But the dawn of the Internet age has introduced some new targeting tactics, all courtesy of your friendly direct-marketing department.

- **Email lists:** You probably provide your email address fairly often, whether you're paying for a subscription, renewing a membership, joining a mailing list, or signing up for a contest. Some companies and publications, reputable and disreputable alike, will sell your email address to other companies looking to target customers who are likely to be interested in their product. If you've just subscribed to a cooking magazine, for example, you might find a subscription offer from an interior-decorating magazine in your inbox.

- **Spam:** Not all companies want to spend the time and money it takes to track down people who are likely to be interested in their product. The result? Spamming potential customers at random by sending them unsolicited emails advertising a product or service.

- **Cookies:** Websites place cookies (identifying numbers) on your computer so that they know when and how often you come back. It's cookies that allow Amazon.com, for example, to welcome you back by name. Some cookies enable companies to track you as you roam around to different websites online.

- **Targeted email ads:** Some email services, notably Gmail, automatically scan the emails you send and receive and run related ads according to the key words you've used. For example, if you write to your friend about a Halloween costume, ads for costume stores will pop up next to your email exchange.

- **Tracked browsing:** Companies such as Yahoo! track their customers' online behavior, noting what ads they click, what sites they visit, and what searches they make, and advertise to them accordingly.

- **Brand marketing:** Managing a brand, such as Tide or UPS, involves conceptualizing and designing logos, working with ad agencies on campaigns, determining the key message to get across during new product launches, and working with the PR team to manage the public's perception of that brand and what it represents (good service, high quality, etc.). Brand marketing requires serious strategic planning and big-picture vision. For this reason, it is among the more competitive areas of marketing, and breaking in can be a challenge. Some larger companies require their brand marketers to have an MBA or at least five years of experience working in advertising or marketing. Internships and networking are a good place to start if you want to angle for a job, and you may have to spend some time in a related capacity before making the jump. But because brand marketers play such a strategic role in surveying the competitive landscape and positioning the company accordingly, the accompanying monetary compensation can be worth the wait.

All marketing departments are fast-paced and intense. To succeed in the field, you'll need to be good at coordinating, managing, communicating, and thinking creatively. You get into marketing in much the same way as advertising: networking, professional organizations, alumni centers, internships, the works. And crossover between the two fields is fairly common.

Public Relations Departments

Public relations is image management. PR departments generate and manage news to keep the public's perception of a company consistent with the message crafted by marketing and promoted through advertising. They do everything from helping a Fortune 500 company get featured on the front page of the *Wall Street Journal*, to spreading the word about the launch of a new online store, to coordinating a free scoop day promotion for an ice cream shop chain. The PR team also helps executives make policy decisions and strategic plans by explaining the likely public response. If ExxonMobil sponsors a nonprofit wildlife organization or supports a bill to limit emissions, it's likely the PR peeps suggested it as a way to promote them as an environmentally friendly company.

PR departments perform many functions and play many roles. Copywriters and corporate communications specialists write internal memos

Addicted to weekly celebrity gossip magazines or read celebrity news blogs? You might be a natural fit for public relations.

about company business ("Here's how to respond to questions about our recent merger"), employee newsletters to entertain and motivate the troops, press releases for news outlets and the company website, fact sheets for industry publications, and event brochures for publicity. Event planners handle the promotional parties, launch events, conferences, trade show appearances, and exhibitions a company uses to keep itself in the public eye. Publicists create buzz about new company developments and communicate with news outlets, highlighting good news and minimizing the damage done by bad news. Depending on the size of the company, these various responsibilities may be handled by an individual or team or by the department as a whole.

66 In the morning, I spend my time monitoring the media: reading newspapers and scanning online to see if my product or anything related to my accounts is mentioned. The rest of the day varies, depending on what I'm working on. I could be pitching to the media—making phone calls and writing emails to give them story ideas—or I could be working research and logistics to plan events or execute tactics that support our campaign."

—**Karissa Chen,** Junior Account Executive
DeVries

Because every industry needs skilled PR people, you'll be able to find work that interests you whether you're a techno-junkie or a Prada-clad fashionista. A degree in journalism, English, or communications can help you get your foot in the door, and proven writing and people skills are always appealing to potential employers, but you'll do most of your learning on the job. Many companies have their own PR departments, but outside PR agencies are a great first stop for entry-level grads, since they provide access to a wide range of clients and products. At the entry level, expect to develop lists of media contacts, track publicity opportunities, manage public-speaking engagements for executives, gather press clippings, monitor news outlets, analyze coverage, write first drafts of press releases, fact sheets, and timelines, and direct traffic from local and regional press. To succeed, you'll need good communication skills and the confidence to perform well under pressure. You'll be asked to make cold calls, meet deadlines, spin great stories from bad material, and maintain a cheerful, professional demeanor no matter what the situation.

Centennial College in Toronto offers an intensive program in corporate communications, which culminates in a two-month placement at a PR agency.

PRWeek is *the* industry magazine for public relations.

Check out the following websites for job listings, workshops, seminars for budding PR professionals, and local networking events:

prsa.org
prnewswire.com
www.iabc.com

Specialized PR firms

PR specialists exist in virtually every industry niche. Here are some of the umbrellas under which these jobs tend to be grouped:

- **Government and public affairs**
  PR has contributed to the success of many government social education programs on issues ranging from drinking and driving to forest fires and the food pyramid. According to *PRWeek*, the firm Edelman recently increased its government PR business by 66 percent, mainly due to the PR it did for stem cell research on behalf of the California Institute for Regenerative Medicine. Another large firm, Fleischman-Hillard, has done communications work for homeland security and the U.S. Army.

- **Food and nutrition**
  As concern about childhood obesity and diabetes grows, consumer packaged goods clients are feeling increased pressure and turning to PR agencies for help. Ketchum, one of the larger PR firms, has a branch that specializes entirely in communications for food and nutrition clients. Its new client acquisitions include Weight Watchers, Ghiradelli Chocolate, and Pepperidge Farms.

- **Healthcare**
  As healthcare and pharmaceutical companies grow, attract competition, and increase public awareness, they need PR agencies. Chandler Chicco Agency, one of the top PR firms in biotech healthcare, has grown significantly and expanded to key Asian markets. Its clients include Genentech, Amgen, Ortho Women's Health, Botox (Allergan), and the American Society of Microbiology.

- **Technology and communications**
  Many PR agencies work solely for online companies. Most of the major tech players have an office in the Bay Area hub of Silicon Valley. The GCI Group has seen terrific growth as a result of its foray into digital entertainment and has recently expanded its presence in northern California. Other major players include Ruder Finn, Weber Shandwick, and, again, Fleischman-Hillard.

Other specialized fields include media, education, and ethnic markets, among others. To learn more, check out the Public Relations Society of America at psra.org.

PR FREELANCING

Many companies use freelancers for corporate communications and copywriting. In particular, smaller companies that don't have the budget for a full-service PR agency often pay freelancers to help them create and implement communications strategies or materials for PR use. The work tends to be fairly straightforward, and companies will come back to a freelancer who makes their deadlines and does a good job of mimicking their voice. Writing an annual report for the California Dental Hygienists' Association might not be the most exciting work in the world, but these opportunities tend to pay well and look great on your résumé.

Though word of mouth is the best way to find freelance work, Craigslist and Mediabistro.com are excellent resources as well. And even if you're living in, say, New York City, check the listings for other parts of the country. A startup in Silicon Valley might want a freelancer based in NYC to communicate with trade publications and potential customers and investors on the East Coast.

EVENT PLANNING

Though often housed under PR, event planning is big enough for many companies and agencies to include as a separate entity. Any event that requires coordination, pizzazz, and originality calls for a crack event-planning team. The free drink and hors d'oeuvres hour at a slick downtown club where screens project abstract, evocative images and a well-tailored individual gives a 10 minute spiel about Absolut's new vodka flavor is all the work of a dedicated, detail-oriented event planner.

This is one job where you'll be judged on your Rolodex. An event planner is essentially a social butterfly. You'll need the stamina to network until your throat is sore, shake hands until your wrist is limp, and smile until your face hurts. You'll gather contacts of all kinds: caterers, security, DJs, publicists for VIPs, restaurant and club managers, and editors and marketers at newspapers and magazines. Event planning is exciting, but it's not all glitz and glamour. To succeed, you'll need to be incredibly organized and possess great project management skills.

Once you've built up an extensive contact list and some solid years of experience under your belt, you might consider flying solo. Many event planners work as independent consultants, performing their magic on a one-off basis. This can be a very lucrative and flexible option, requiring minimal staff and giving you complete control of a project.

66 I worked in event planning for a major magazine, and one of our events was a huge business conference on an island off the coast of Michigan. My job was to greet guests flying into a tiny airport and direct them to a ferry that would take them to their accommodations. When the last flight arrived, holding a CEO, a professional basketball, and one of our keynote speakers, the weather was so horrendous that the ferry would not take us. We ended up eating dinner at Denny's and sleeping in a Motel 8, where the bed was *waaay* too small for the NBA player!

—**Randi Zuckerberg,** former Account Executive
Forbes Conference Group

Sales Departments

If advertising is a one-way message delivery service, sales is a two-way consultation. Salespeople sell Pepsi to grocery stores, airplanes to Jet Blue, and magazine space to advertisers. They are the ones who persuade buyers, be it a company, store, or other commercial establishment, to part with their dime in exchange for a great product or service. It's the personal, intimate, and friendly piece of the marketing mix.

Salespeople have two key responsibilities: to represent the company by identifying and working with clients and to represent the customer by communicating client concerns back to the company. Salespeople are spokespeople and liaisons. They are the chauffeurs on the highway of commerce, driving deals start to finish, making sure customers are satisfied and encouraged to come back for more. Because so much in sales depends on the ability to develop good relationships, companies choose their sales reps wisely. Anytime there's turnover or a rep does poorly, the customer relationship suffers, which can hurt company revenue. When hiring, companies tend to rely on recommendations from trusted reps, inside people working for other departments, employment agencies, and scouting of the competitor's sales force. Many companies administer tests to determine the analytical skills, personality traits, and sales aptitude of potential salespeople.

A successful salesperson is motivated, confident, and charismatic. You'll need to feel comfortable selling people things they might not know they want or need. You need the chutzpah to keep pitching your company's product even after your potential customer has just said "no" to your face. And you need a high tolerance for stress, especially when the end of the quarter is approaching and you're short of your quota. At the entry level, you probably won't be out on the front lines, meeting with clients and selling millions of dollars' worth in products or services. Instead, you'll likely provide support for one or more sales representatives. The research you do, the data you organize, and the presentations you put together will be integral to the reps' success. Though every company handles sales in its own way, departments are usually split between the outside and inside sales teams.

Check out salesjobs.com and marketingjobs.com for job postings, career advice, and recruiting services.

OUTSIDE SALES REPS

Outside sales reps spend most of their working day in the field, that is, away from the office. Outside sales reps make personal calls to a relatively small number of high-paying clients and get to know them well. The biggest accounts will generally go to senior salespeople with terrific reputations, whom the company trusts to negotiate those deals that can bring in substantial revenue.

A talented rep can make a great deal of money between base salary and commission. This potentially lucrative career path also offers perks such as expense accounts, travel opportunities, tickets to cool events in the name of client development, and lots of free stuff from the clients you work with. Outside sales is fun and flashy, but it's also stressful. Factors out of your control, such as adverse industry trends or economic downturns, can destabilize you. A tough quarter can mean low income and potential job loss. And the end-of-quarter rush to earn as much revenue as possible can be murder.

INSIDE SALES REPS

Inside sales reps conduct business from the friendly confines of their desk and often act as a buffer to reduce the time spent by outside reps on lower-revenue clients. Technical support people, sales assistants, and

Inside sales also includes the sales director, who oversees the entire sales force, inside and outside, and regional sales managers, who supervise the outside reps in a specific region.

telemarketers are all included in this group. You'll have revenue goals, but they're significantly lower than those of outside reps. And as an inside rep, you'll conduct most of your business over the phone rather than traveling to do it in person. The work entails a high volume of customers reached through a variety of situations, and technology has added to the complexity. You may be asked to answer customer emails or contribute to FAQ pages on a company website. This may not sound as glamorous as dinner at a five-star restaurant or tickets to a Lakers game, but what you lose in perks, you gain in knowledge. Inside sales is a terrific way to gain experience and work your way up to your dream job in outside sales.

RELATED CAREER FIELDS

Advertising and marketing aren't the only fields that focus on conveying a message with creativity and imagination. If you're looking for a field where your communication, design, or language skills will be valued, consider book, magazine, and online publishing. The roles in this industry are as varied as those in advertising. Here we'll focus on some of the more creative options.

Book Publishing

Compared to advertising or even other areas of publishing, book publishing operates at a stately pace. Rather than late-breaking developments and last-second changes, you're working with writers who may take years to complete their manuscripts (though last-second changes aren't unheard of). Despite its sometimes slow tempo, the book-publishing experience is a challenging and rewarding one. Here are some of the departments you might consider.

EDITORIAL DEPARTMENTS

The editor oversees the process of transforming a manuscript into a bound book form, a process that can take anywhere from one to several years. As an editor, you have a hands-on role in shaping the manuscript into a marketable and readable product. You work with the author on refining the manuscript, the designer on cover and interior design, and the sales, marketing, and publicity departments on copy and promotional materials. Editors in book publishing get a firsthand glimpse of the creative-writing process—a prospect most wordsmiths relish. This means that an editorial job can be a great learning experience for budding authors.

The most sought-after entry-level position in the book-publishing industry is that of editorial assistant (EA). The job involves demanding, sometimes menial, but rewarding work. You'll read the pile of unsolicited manuscripts, identifying and writing reports on the more promising ones and passing them along to the editor for review. To determine the value of manuscripts, you'll check the competition and provide summaries of any similar books. You'll also handle the administrative and clerical work for the entire editorial department, including answering phones and mail, taking minutes at editorial meetings, filing, photocopying, managing the schedules and transit of materials to other departments, and mailing manuscripts and proofs to authors for review.

To land a job, scour publishing house job listings and websites such as mediabistro.com and bookjobs.com. The larger companies list jobs on their websites. Editors have been known to hire promising recent grads with little to no experience as EAs, but it always helps if you have a connection in the field. Better your chances of getting hired full-time by taking unpaid internships, which are a sure way of getting your foot in the door and your face in front of editors.

BOOK DESIGN

As long as books are printed, the world of book publishing will need designers. In our visual culture, knockout book jackets make all the difference. A book with a killer cover and a third-rate story will often sell better than a book with a boring cover that hides a masterpiece. Interior design is just as crucial: Clunky typography and sloppy text breaks can be enough to make a bookstore browser return that novel to the shelf.

The major challenge for a designer is expressing written content in a visual way. And as with creatives in advertising, to get hired, you'll

Publishing industry must reads: *Publisher's Weekly* and *Publisher's Lunch,* a free newsletter from publishers marketplace. com.

CHAPTER 8: EXPLORING RELATED OPPORTUNITIES

The most famous jacket designer is Chip Kidd. His book, *Chip Kidd: Book One—Work: 1986–2006,* offers a fascinating glimpse into the commercial application of an artist's mind.

need to get yourself noticed by displaying your work. It's crucial to have a full portfolio that shows your range, both artistically and technically. Do you have a favorite book that you almost didn't pick up because the cover was so bad? Take a few hours (or a day, or a week) and design an alternate cover. You won't get far as a one-trick pony, even if your trick is the best on the block. So read books, design jackets, put together a killer résumé, and get on those job boards.

Magazine Publishing

Magazines, or "glossies" as they're called on the inside, are the perfect place to use your writing or designing skills in a fast-paced, energetic environment. Because magazines make money through their circulations, including subscribers and impulse buyers, working in the industry requires an almost clairvoyant understanding of trends. Unfortunately, working in magazine publishing means long hours and so-so pay. But it also means producing a product that lots of people will read and enjoy.

In this book, you've read about magazines as a media outlet for advertisers. If you're interested in keeping your hand in advertising, you can aim for a position in media sales. But if you're interested in other aspects of the industry, consider the roles available for editors, writers, and designers.

Finding work

Here are a couple of places to spot potential openings in magazine publishing:

Mediabistro.com: Mediabistro.com's daily "Revolving Door" feature gives instant updates as to the comings and goings of magazine staffers. Keep track of its postings, and you can get a head start on your résumé before the jilted magazine even posts a job listing.

Ed2010, ed2010.com: Ed2010's "whisper" listings are similar to mediabistro.com's "Revolving Door," with an added bonus: "Whispers" are posted as soon as a rumor starts going around. The rumor might not be true, but if it is, you'll be the very first in line for a job. Well, along with everyone else reading the site.

EDITORIAL DEPARTMENTS

The editorial department lies at the heart of a magazine. People in editorial are responsible for crafting the prose that hundreds or thousands of readers encounter each week or month. The tone and pace at a weekly news rag is very different from that at, for example, a monthly fashion mag, but the editorial process is similar everywhere. Writers and editors pitch ideas to an editor in chief or editorial board and gather in weekly staff meetings. Editors assign stories to specific writers, who do research, conduct interviews, and write. Editors and writers go back and forth, inching the piece along toward its final form. (As a general rule: The bigger the magazine, the less input the writer has once a piece is submitted.) Editors collaborate with art and design to put together each issue.

The entry-level position here is also editorial assistant. Duties and responsibilities vary drastically from magazine to magazine. Some EAs write, proofread, and report. Others fetch dry cleaning, answer phones, and do clerical tasks. Most EAs have some prior experience, whether as a freelance writer, a college newspaper columnist, an intern, or an employee at a publishing house or another magazine. Salaries aren't terrific, but some magazines offer you overtime pay and perks such as invitations to parties and any free stuff the editors decide to pass on. Most newbies work at the EA level for two to three years before moving up, although that number varies depending on the company and your skills.

FREELANCE WRITING

Some magazine articles are written by in-house editors and contributing editors, but most are by freelance writers. These writers come up with a story idea, do research, and then pitch the idea to an editor via a query letter. Sometimes an editor will contact an established writer with a story idea, but many published stories begin as freelance pitches. If an editor likes a pitch, he'll hire the writer to do the story. He'll give the writer a word count, work with her to fine-tune the idea, and edit the prose once the piece is complete.

As a freelancer, you need to be comfortable with rejection. For every *yes* you hear, you'll hear 50 *nos*. The pitching process can be competitive, especially at the higher-end publications. And it can be tough to refill the well with fresh story ideas that appeal to editors and readers. To get started writing for magazines, you'll need to collect clips (samples of your published articles). If you don't have clips from your school paper or magazine, start by writing to a local paper or magazine. In a brief, polite letter, explain why your idea is worth pursuing and why you're the ideal writer to pursue it. Your query letter is an advertisement for your writing skills and your idea, so make sure it's grammatically impeccable and pleasant to read. An internship with a magazine may also give you the chance to write, not to mention the valuable contacts and knowledge about the field you'll gain.

66 Freelance writing is the ideal job for writers with widely varying interests and an appetite for deadline work in pajamas. I love working at home, because I find it much more efficient than going into the office—I gain two hours a day by skipping the commute and outfits alone—and I get to hang out with my pooch all day. I can also work for a wide variety of men's, women's, and general-interest publications at the same time, which is great for my peripatetic interests. You already know the work schedule—it's like college."

—**Arianne Cohen,** Freelancer for the *New York Times, Nerve.com,* and *Marie Claire,* among others

ART, PHOTO, AND DESIGN

Behind every successful magazine is a dynamic art department that makes the pages pop and zing. Employees in the art department need to be skilled visual artists. They also need the ability to maintain a consistent aesthetic and to make a magazine's appearance reflect its editorial sensibility. The casual reader looks at a page in a magazine and sees a collection of words and images, but artists and designers look at the same page and see possibilities for spreads that enhance the content of the article and add to the reading experience.

As with editorial departments, the atmosphere of art and design departments varies according to the magazine's subject matter and parent company. At a fashion magazine, where images mean everything, the art and design departments will be run more tightly than at a literary or news magazine, where photos aren't quite as important. Art and design departments also tend to feel more collaborative than other departments. Art and photo staffers arrange photo shoots, secure the rights to images, and

Many visual-arts-oriented schools offer summer or evening classes. Check out artschools.com for a directory of over 3,500 art schools across the country and start creating.

pass those images along to designers, who integrate the art with words from editorial. As in the editorial department, entry-level jobs in art, design, and photo departments are assistant positions, either for a particular person or for the entire department. Art-side newbies do a lot of grunt work, such as photocopying, scanning images, and calling to confirm appointments. The longer they stay, the more responsibility they get.

There have always been more talented designers than there are design positions. But because advances in technology have made formerly complicated, expensive computer programs widely accessible, competition in the industry is fiercer than ever. As more and more recent grads embrace technology, build their own websites, and create their own blogs, you can't swing a mouse in an empty room without hitting someone with graphic design experience. And many full-time designers and art and photo directors do freelance work to fill their portfolios and their pockets, cutting down further on the number of available jobs. Still, talented people will be able to find work. Technology has changed the industry, but ingenuity, taste, and artistic talent are still in high demand. Art, photo, and design are highly specialized fields. Landing an entry-level job will require a strong portfolio and a working knowledge of photo and design techniques, styles, technology, and formats.

Online Publishing

Now that almost every publication has an online component, almost every publication needs a web guru or five. Editing, writing, and designing online content requires exactly the same facility with grammar, style, and prose as editing and writing for magazines and books, but it tends to work at a much quicker pace. It also requires an understanding of the Internet and the reading habits of your site's visitors. You must present information so that readers come to the site in the first place and hang around once they get there. Websites make money by selling advertising, and advertisers want to spend money on sites that attract lots of frequent and lingering visitors.

If you want to work on websites, you need to know programming languages such as XTML or Dreamweaver and understand applications and content management systems. You also need to see the big picture and figure out how to get other sites to link to yours. If you need to bone up on these basic skills, take a class in web design or programming and create your own website to get some practice.

CONTENT CREATORS

Because limits on space and accessibility (for both publishers and consumers) are virtually nonexistent on the web and publication is nearly instantaneous, this can be a great place for a budding writer to publish his work. Stories written for the web tend to be shorter and punchier than those written for the printed page, and since online-publishing schedules roll on a minute-by-minute basis, there's an endless need for content. The editorial process differs from site to site, but in general, web writing follows a less stringent path to publication than books or magazines. This means the content that makes its way to the viewer's eyes is more likely to be the writer's exact words than a heavily edited and chopped-up version, for better or worse.

In addition to the many online-only publications, most print magazines also produce daily content for their websites apart from what's printed. Because of the constant need to fill the virtual page, web publishers are more willing to take chances on untested writers. If you have a knack for concise, punchy writing and 50-word blurbs, get in touch with the web editors of your favorite magazines' sites and suggest they take you on as a guest blogger. Or call them up and pitch a longer story idea.

WEB DESIGNERS

Web design can mean anything from performing a purely technical operation (say, building a database) to creating a fully integrated website that represents a company's services and identity. Successful web designers will have both technical and artistic skills. If you're a great logo designer but can't program Flash to save your life, take a quick class or get a tutorial from a friend. If you're an HTML hound but feel a little rusty on layouts, do some practice runs and refine your craft.

If you're talented and have good connections, you won't have trouble scoring consistent work. To get hired, you'll need a portfolio. If you're short of samples, consider doing pro bono jobs to build up your book. Create a website of your own, or find someone who wants to create or spruce up their own site. Companies might not know they need a new website until you tell them they do. Web design is such a rapidly evolving field that they may not know what's possible. Look around online and find sites that need work. Then, in a courteous email, approach their directors with free tips and a brief explanation of what you would do for their website if hired. Your suggestions for moving parts and a podcast might inspire them to write you a check or at least give you a shot at a redesign.

PART III: CAREER-PLANNING TOOLS

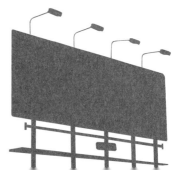

FURTHER RESOURCES

BOOKS

Advertising: Concept and Copy, by George Felton, Norton, 2005
Though focused on copywriting, this textbook offers a great survey of
the strategies and tricks of the trade necessary for success in advertising,
including commentary on the changes in mass media, guerrilla marketing,
and the international advertising landscape.

**The Art of Writing Advertising: Conversations with Masters of the
Craft: David Ogilvy, William Bernbach, Leo Burnett, Rosser Reeves,
and George Gribbin,** by Denis Higgins, McGraw-Hill, 2003
A collection of interviews that *Advertising Age* conducted in the 60s with
four of the biggest names in advertising at the time, the wisdom dispensed
in these pages is just as relevant for today's professionals. Filled with wit
and personality, this books provides insight into how you create a great ad,
straight from the horses' mouths.

The Book of Gossage, by Howard Luck Gossage, The Copy Workshop, 1995
Gossage was a pioneer in the '50s and '60s and is considered by many
to have changed the face of advertising through his consumer-driven
approach. Essays written by Gossage, "The Socrates of San Francisco," as
he was known, and others whom he's influenced, reveal the man and
his philosophy.

A Century of American Icons, by Mary Cross, Greenwood Publishing
Group, 2002
This book details the top ad campaigns and slogans that defined the consumer culture throughout each decade of the twentieth century. A great
survey of influential ads and an informative chronicle of the consumer
culture in America.

Confessions of an Advertising Man, by David Ogilvy, Atheneum, 1976
Ogilvy on Advertising, by David Ogilvy, Crown, 1983
David Ogilvy has penned numerous books, both personal and technical, on
the world of advertising. Although any one of them will give you a deeper
understanding of the business, these two are considered must-reads. Both

provide wisdom and inspiration, as well as some practical know-how from the "father of modern advertising."

The End of Advertising as We Know It, by Sergio Zyman, Wiley, 2002
A look at the failures and shortcomings in recent advertising, this book attacks some of the most recognized campaigns of late. Zyman's critique is leveled at current advertising and marketing strategies that aim to create a buzz at the expense of promoting products and services. An eye-opening read from a longtime marketing guru.

Guerrilla Advertising, by Jay Conrad Levinson, Charles Rubin, Houghton Mifflin, 1994
Levinson has penned countless books on practical marketing and advertising strategies. _Guerrilla Advertising_ is a great how-to resource for conceiving, planning, and implementing creative advertising campaigns that are effective and thrifty.

The Little Blue Book of Advertising: 52 Small Ideas That Can Make a Big Difference, by Steve Lance, Jeff Woll, Penguin, 2006
A handy handbook on what works and what doesn't from two former creative directors. _The Little Blue Book of Advertising_ is light on theory and heavy on practical tips, making for an easy read that can be referred to again and again.

Permission Marketing, by Seth Godin, Simon & Schuster, 1999
By that famous author-cum-blogger Seth Godin, this popular and influential book encourages advertisers and marketers to "get a consumer's permission" by offering a hook or incentive, thereby solidifying a long-term relationship. Seth Godin has many books, but this is arguably the one to read.

Then We Set His Hair on Fire: Insights and Accidents from a Hall-of-Fame Career in Advertising, by Phil Dusenberry, Penguin, 2005
A practical, informative, and hugely entertaining memoir from the BBDO exec and industry legend, this book provides insight into creating ads that sell a brand for generations from a man who has had more than his share of them.

Twenty Ads That Shook the World: The Century's Most Groundbreaking Advertising and How It Changed Us All, by James B. Twitchell, Crown, 2000

Both insightful and entertaining, Twitchell presents the most successful and recognizable campaigns of the past century, from "Just Do It" to the Marlboro Man, and plumbs the creative and psychological forces at work behind them.

PROFESSIONAL RESOURCES

The **Advertising Age** ***Encyclopedia of Advertising,*** Routledge, 2002

This three-volume resource includes detailed profiles of over 100 ad agencies around the world, essays on the industry, biographies of major players, and bios on significant Fortune 500 advertisers, as well as information on leading brands and campaigns.

The One Show Annual, The One Show Club, annual publication

Annual catalog of the year's best in creative advertising as spotlighted in the One Show Awards. This glossy, full-color text includes illustrations of the ads along with in-depth comments from the judges. A staple in most creative departments.

Standard Directory of Advertisers **("The Red Book"),** National Register Publishing, annual publication

Better known as "the advertising bible," this is by far the most comprehensive printed source on thousands of ad agencies nationwide, including data on clients and top executives. Owning this book requires a substantial chunk of change, though, so you're better off using your local library's edition.

TRADE PUBLICATIONS

The Advertiser, ana.net/advertiser/advertiser.htm
This bimonthly magazine, published by the Association of National Advertisers, provides news and insights on the best brand-building and marketing strategies.

Advertising Age, adage.com
Weekly tabloid newspaper–style magazine that covers industry news, including the latest on campaigns, people and players, new media, and account action.

Adweek, adweek.com
Weekly magazine covering all the hottest news in the advertising industry. Covers accounts in review, agency/client relationships, industry executives, and the freshest campaigns and creative names.

Brandweek, brandweek.com
Adweek's counterpart for the marketing industry. For advertising professionals, this is a great resource for staying up on what's happening in the greater marketing world. Learn about everything from big-budget full-service agency ad campaigns to take-it-to-the-streets, low-budget guerrilla marketing campaigns.

BtoB Magazine, btobonline.com
The source for business-to-business marketing. Published monthly by Crain Communications, who also own *Advertising Age, BtoB* includes articles and detailed information on marketing strategy.

Creativity, adcritic.com
Another one from Crain Communications, *Creativity* is a monthly magazine that can be a great resource for creatives and anyone else interested in the creative side of advertising. Along with the latest news and profiles of people in the field, there are informative articles on the cultural landscape of the advertising world. *Creativity*'s online arm, adcritic.com, contains additional content beyond what you'll find in the printed magazine.

Journal of Advertising, www.bus.iastate.edu/joa
Combining theory with practical application, this academic journal will open a side of advertising that's more philosophical, ethical, and sociological than you'll find in some of the other mainstream publications.

one. a magazine, oneclub.com
one is a great resource for anyone working on the creative side. Each issue includes interviews with the industry's best and brightest creative minds, articles on hot trends, and behind-the-scenes looks into the making of ads.

Cultural glitter-acy

Knowing which celebrities, movies, and cultural trends are hot is important for anyone trying to influence pop culture. Keep yourself in the know with these newsstand favorites. Remember, the consumer's doing the same thing:

Magazines: *PREMIERE, Us Weekly, Entertainment Weekly*

Websites: gawker.com, salon.com, nerve.com

Blogs: perezhilton.com, socialitelife.com, jossip.com, dailyblabber. ivillage.com (really, there are too many to list them all!)

PROFESSIONAL ASSOCIATIONS

Ad Brands, www.mind-advertising.com
A great resource for profiles on hundreds of brands and ad agencies worldwide.

Ad Council, adcouncil.org
The leading producer of public service announcements; visit the Ad Council website to see creative work from its social-awareness ad campaign, dating to the 1940s, or to get involved (they recruit volunteers from all over the advertising community!).

The Advertising Club of New York, theadvertisingclub.org
The Advertising Club is an organization that promotes networking
and idea sharing among professionals working in marketing and advertising. Through their philanthropic arm, The Foundation, the club assists
students in finding internships and work in advertising and related fields.

Advertising Educational Foundation, aef.com
The AEF is a nonprofit organization dedicated to providing students and
professors, and anyone else who's interested, with educational content to
inform and expand the advertising discourse. The AEF provides classroom
and teaching resources, hosts on-campus events, and provides career-
building services, including news on industry leaders, job hunting advice,
and links to job-posting sites.

American Advertising Federation, www.aaf.org
The AAF is a trade association that represents the people who make up the
industry. With thousands of members, the AAF conducts programs, holds
summits, hosts award shows, and provides a great outlet for networking
and industry education.

American Association of Advertising Agencies, www.aaaa.org
Better known as the Four A's, the AAAA is the national trade association
representing advertising agencies. Most of the large, full-service agencies
in the country are members. The website features general info, as well as
members-only materials and events.

American Business Media, americanbusinessmedia.com
The ABM is an association of more than 300 business media companies. It
sponsors the Business Press Educational Foundation Summer Internship
program, which places undergrad and grad students in paid positions at a
variety of business-to-business publications.

Association of National Advertisers, ana.net
The ANA provides insight, strategic support, and advocacy in brand marketing
tactics to member companies as diverse as JP Morgan Chase, the Ford Motor
Company, Office Depot, and the California Lottery. Among their many objec-
tives is to "be the most powerful and influential marketing organization to

lead industry initiatives, to influence industry practices, to manage industry affairs, and to advance, promote and protect all advertisers and marketers."

International Advertising Association, iaaglobal.org

An international advertising advocacy group, IAA is committed to "fight unwarranted regulation on behalf of all those engaged in responsible commercial speech and to act as an advocate for freedom of choice for individuals across all consumer and business markets." This site is also a great place to find out about news, events, agency profiles, and job searches across the industry worldwide.

Internet Advertising Bureau, iab.net

The IAB is a major association dedicated to online advertising and marketing. It has created the standard for Internet advertising and serves as a great resource for any professional on the interactive side of the industry.

Media Watch, mediawatch.com

Media Watch is an advocacy group that challenges the stereotyping and bias commonly found in media. Through public awareness campaigns and activism, the group has been an influential voice during their 20-plus years of existence. Its website is a great source for news you might not find elsewhere.

New York American Marketing Association, nyama.org

The NYAMA is an organization of professional marketers and advertisers working across the globe. They host events, provide industry directories, and host a job search site.

The One Club, oneclub.com

This group of industry creatives gathers for the purpose of discourse and education in innovative advertising strategies. Their annual One Show Awards are a highly anticipated event among industry creatives.

Outdoor Advertising Association of America, oaaa.org

The leading trade organization for outdoor advertising, the OAAA advocates for over 1,100 members. The OAAA has a strong government policy presence and the website is a great source for news, events, and research on this advertising niche.

Websites and Blogs

AdAge, adage.com

The latest and greatest in the advertising industry. If it's not mentioned on this website, it probably doesn't matter. This is a great place to keep up on breaking industry news, account wins and losses, and the best creative work out there.

AdBase, adbase.com

Adbase is a clearinghouse organization for companies searching for creative work, and it's also a great place to gather names of specialist agencies of all shapes and sizes.

Ad Forum, adforum.com

A great source for news on the global ad industry, Ad Forum is used by companies in search of agencies and provides info tons of info on ads and agencies.

Adrants, adrants.com

Up-to-the-moment advertising and marketing news with honest, biting commentary on the state of business today. Published by an ad industry insider, the site offers a popular daily newsletter, nationwide job listings, and an easy-to-navigate content list arranged by subject.

Adweek, adweek.com

This subscription-based website is the online portal to *Adweek* magazine, a trade magazine widely read throughout the industry. Subscribers will get inside info on industry news, exciting account transfers, and award-winning production. Be sure to check out the AdFreak blog as well, at adweek.blogs.com.

Brandweek, brandweek.com

A great source for the latest in marketing news. Brandweek.com covers news on the corporate and agency level for marketing strategies, branding identify, licensing issues, media usage and distribution, and more.

Hoover's, hoovers.com

A terrific resource to find information on thousands of publicly and privately held companies around the world. You can expect to find links to company websites, annual financial reports, main competitors, and industry information. Be warned, however, that the best information only comes with an expensive paid subscription to the Hoover's service.

I Want Media, iwantmedia.com

A blog source for daily all-media business news, from books to newspapers to magazines to web journalism.

Mediabistro.com

This is a who's who in media. The site has everything from job postings to industry news. You can also find info on who in the industry is moving on through the revolving door, including who has recently switched jobs, been promoted, and all that juicy stuff.

MediaWeek, mediaweek.com

An industry resource covering all facets of the media business, including television, the Internet, newspapers, and magazines.

Seth Godin's Blog, sethgodin.typepad.com

Industry author Seth Godin, who has become somewhat of a household name, writes this very popular marketing blog that has the commentary on everything remotely having to do with marketing and human nature, really.

VNU eMedia, vnuemedia.com

This site contains links to many daily advertising and marketing newsletters, making it a great one-stop shop to find information about the industry.

JOB LISTINGS AND RECRUITERS

Adecco Creative, adeccocreative.com

A subdivision of the international recruiter Adecco, this group was founded not too long ago as a creative services provider. It caters to many markets, including publishing, advertising, and public relations. A great source for prospective art directors and copywriters.

CollegeGrad, collegegrad.com

A priceless resource exclusively for college students and recent college graduates. This award-winning site provides the most comprehensive entry-level job search content of any job site on the Internet.

Craigslist, newyork.craigslist.org, boston.craigslist.org, etc.

Looking for a job, apartment, or freelance work? Try Craigslist, the nation's bulletin board. Pick your city, then cruise to the job section.

Greenberg Kirshenbaum, greenbergkirshenbaum.com

This New York–based recruitment firm locates permanent and freelance opportunities for creative talent in advertising and new media agencies worldwide.

Indeed, indeed.com
Meta-job-posting site that searches most of the leading career sites and pulls data on open positions into one place.

Jobster, jobster.com
This Web 2.0 site connects thousands of job seekers and employers for career matches in virtually every industry, including marketing and advertising.

Lynne Palmer Executive Recruitment, lynnepalmerinc.com
Since 1964, this agency has been placing qualified people into jobs throughout marketing and media industries. A great place for assistance with creative, sales, account manager, PR, and media positions at agencies nationwide.

Mediabistro.com
Probably the best site on the web for jobs in publishing and other media fields. Mediabistro is the media professional's answer to Monster.com. The site features job postings, industry resources, and forums, as well as posts information about networking events, classes, and career development seminars.

Monster, monster.com
The leading job-posting site on the net, Monster has career information and job postings for every possible industry, including a robust section for advertising and media careers.

Ribolow Associates, ribolow.com
This recruiting agency specializes in the advertising and publishing industries. Its sister company, Ribolow Staffing Services, also provides temporary work for professionals in transition.

Talent Zoo, talentzoo.com
Voted by *Forbes* magazine as one of the best media job-posting sites on the web, Talent Zoo has many job postings for account management and creative services, for both ad agencies and the client side of things.

INDUSTRY GLOSSARY

account management: The department responsible for closely managing the relationship between a client and an agency or media company. Account management acts as a liaison between the client and other agency departments, such as creative or media services.

added value: Extra ad units or additional discounts given to a media buyer or advertiser in exchange for purchasing a large amount of ad placements. Also know as a *horizontal discount*.

advertising: Paid form of mass communication, designed to persuade the consumer to take a specific action. Advertising generally comes from an identifiable source, i.e., the company producing the good or service.

advertising unit: Specific placement and duration for an ad on a website.

affirmative disclosure: Disclosure of information in an ad as required by the Federal Trade Commission. This information typically indicates limitations or cautions, i.e., the small print.

agency: Company that creates and sometimes produces advertising for a client. They may also provide market research.

American Advertising Federation (AAF): The oldest trade association for advertising, AAF also represents professionals in the business and provide information, news, and resources (aaf.org).

American Association of Advertising Agencies (AAAA): Often referred to as the Four As, this national trade association represents advertising agencies. AAAA's website includes a host of information on the industry and specific agencies, as well as news and conference and seminar announcements. It also runs a famous multicultural internship program (aaaa.org).

animatics: Rough animated sketches, sometimes accompanied by a soundtrack, done prior to filming and used to demonstrate what a final ad will look like.

art director: Person working directly with a copywriter to develop the visual component of an ad campaign.

audience: Number of people exposed to an advertisement, regardless of whether they actually processed the information.

banner advertisement: Visual ad unit appearing on a webpage, generally linked to the website of the company advertised.

billboard: (1) Outdoor sign or poster; (2) sponsor identification at the beginning or end of a television show.

body copy: Text of a print ad, not including the headline, logo, or subscript material.

bonus impressions: In print and online advertising, additional impressions given to an advertiser above the amount outlined in the *insertion order* initially placed with the media vendor.

book: See *portfolio.*

boutique: Ad agency providing a limited service, such as one that does creative work but does not provide media planning, etc., as compared to a full-service agency. Usually refers to a smaller advertising agency.

brand manager: Marketer responsible for managing the image and promotion of a specific brand.

business-to-business advertising: Communications between companies, as opposed to communication directed to consumers.

circulation: Estimated number of copies distributed of a publication. For outdoor advertising this refers to the total number of people who have seen a particular billboard or poster.

click-through rate (CTR): Percentage of people who click on a specific web advertisement.

client: When used by an ad agency, the company that an agency services.

Clio: Annual award given for excellence in advertising (clioawards.com).

collateral: Sales brochures, catalogs, and other printed materials delivered to media buyers or advertisers by a media outlet sales rep to supplement a sales pitch for a specific website, publication, or station.

comparative advertising: Advertising approach consisting of explicit comparisons between two or more competing brands.

copy: Spoken words or written text used in an advertisement.

copy testing: Prior to the launch of a campaign, research using consumer response to determine effectiveness, likability, and potential action created by an ad.

copywriter: Person responsible for creating and overseeing all copy in an advertisement.

corrective advertising: Advertisements the Federal Trade commission requires a company to run to correct consumers' mistaken impressions created by previous advertising.

cost efficiency: In media planning, relative balance of effectively meeting goals of audience exposure at the lowest possible price.

cost per click (CPC): Arrangement between an advertiser and a web company in which an advertiser pays based on the amount of people who clicked on their advertisement.

cost per thousand (CPM): Most often seen in media planning, cost per 1,000 people reached to purchase advertising space in a given media outlet.

creative brief: Document provided to copywriters and art directors outlining the specific message to convey, to whom it is intended, and with what tone it should be created for an advertising campaign.

creatives: An ad agency's *art directors* and *copywriters*.

demographics: Classification of consumers on the basis of descriptors such as age, gender, income, education level, size of household, and job.

direct marketing: Promotional message sent directly to individual consumers, as opposed to advertisements than target a mass audience. Includes methods such as *direct mail* (a marketing piece delivered via mail) and *telemarketing* (solicited or unsolicited calling to prospective consumers).

dog-and-pony show: Elaborate *pitch* or presentation by an advertiser of a campaign concept to a client. Can be either in search of a new business account or for a campaign already commissioned.

dummy: Rough layout of the ad to be produced.

earned rate: Discounted rate, based on purchasing a higher volume of media placement.

engagement: Term used to describe consumer behavior on the Internet. A website is considered having high engagement if users spend a great deal of time on it, interacting with content or other users. The widely held belief in advertising is that an ad placed on a website with high engagement is likely to have greater reach and impact.

envelope stuffer: Direct-mail advertisement included with another mailed message, such as a bill.

estimate: Proposed cost of an advertising effort.

exposure: Number of consumers who may have contact with an advertisement, regardless of whether they processed the information.

flighting: Media schedule where more advertising is launched at certain times and less during others.

focus group: Market research where a group of potential consumers is brought together to discuss a product or advertising of a product under the guidance of a trained interviewer.

fold: Position of an ad on a webpage or newspaper. If a user sees the ad as soon as the page appears, the ad is "above the fold." If the user has to scroll down to see the ad, it is "below the fold."

freelancer: Self-employed person hired by a company for a single project or on a limited-time basis, usually stipulated by a contract or agreement.

freestanding insert: Printed advertisement loosely inserted in a publication, usually offering a promotion or coupon.

frequency: Number of times a person is exposed to an advertising message within a given time.

full-service agency: An agency that handles all aspects of the advertising process.

gatefold: Oversized print pages, generally bound into a magazine, which fold out into a larger advertisement.

graphic design: Artistic rendering or illustration, usually created by an art director.

Greek copy: Gibberish or nonsense text used in place of final copy for layout purposes.

guerrilla marketing: Unconventional marketing techniques, such as T-shirt giveaways or stealthy online blog postings, designed to reach consumers during their daily activities and create buzz. The impact of guerrilla marketing is hard to measure, though these efforts tend to be lower budget than traditional advertising and marketing.

holding company: Umbrella company that owns many communications companies, including advertising agencies (full-service, boutiques, or specialty agencies), media companies, marketing and public relations firms, and market research companies.

hook: Clever, pithy line or melody intended to seize the consumer's attention by making an advertisement more memorable.

horizontal discount: Discount on a media purchase resulting from a promise to advertise over an extended period. See also *added value*.

house agency: Advertising agency owned and operated by a company to manage advertising for its products or services. Also known as *in-house agency*.

impact: Measure of how successfully an advertising campaign reaches the consumer.

impression: In online advertising, term describing each instance an ad is displayed with the potential to be seen. Used to determine costs in media purchases.

insert: Ad inserted into a print publication or direct-mail piece.

insertion order: Specific date and price at which a media company is authorized by an agency to run an ad.

integrated marketing communications (IMC): Integrated and coordinated efforts of a company to deliver a clear and consistent message about its products and/or services.

Interactive Advertising Bureau (IAB): Trade association devoted to the use and effectiveness of interactive advertising and marketing.

interactive marketing: Applies to the emerging world of online/Internet advertising.

international advertising: Advertising conducted in a country outside of where that company is based.

jingle: Short, memorable song, usually mentioning a brand or product, used in a commercial.

key word: Word entered into an Internet website or search engine that produces a list of weblinks for the user. Advertisers can arrange for key word search results to deliver a specific link or message when entered.

launch: Introduction of a new product, service, or campaign.

layout: Design that roughly indicates what an ad will look like.

leaderboard: Short, wide ad unit appearing at the top of a website.

leave-behind: Materials or goods left by a salesperson to remind prospective customers of products or services being sold.

logo: Recognizable lettering style, typeface, or image representing a company or product.

loyalty program: Program created to encourage use of a company's products or services by enticing consumers with a reward for frequent usage (i.e., airline frequent-flyer programs, credit card points).

Madison Avenue: Named after the actual avenue, the area of New York City that has historically been the site of many advertising agencies.

marketing communications mix: Combined efforts of advertising, sales, public relations, and marketing that a company uses to achieve its goal of reaching consumers. Also known as *promotion mix*.

market research: Study of consumer groups, trends, and competition; used to define a product or projected market.

market share: Percentage of a product's sales, compared to competitors', in terms of dollars or units.

media buyer: Person responsible for obtaining space on television, print, and online media outlets for an advertisement.

media plan: Plan for reaching the target market for an advertising campaign through a coordinated effort of media selection and scheduling.

media planner: Person responsible for researching and planning the coordinated media efforts necessary for a given campaign.

medium (plural, media): General category of mass communication used to convey an advertising message, such as television, websites, or magazines.

microsite: Advertiser-specific area of a website designed to look like actual content and often containing interactive elements, such as quizzes and polls, to engage users with a message or content.

mock-up: Display model used in planning to demonstrate what a finished ad will look like.

net cost: Costs for producing an advertisement or campaign, excluding ad agency commission.

Nielsen rating: System to determine U.S. household television viewing of particular shows at particular times. Developed by the Nielsen Media Research firm.

outdoor advertising: Outdoor signage publicly promoting a product or service, e.g., billboards, flyers, and posters.

out-of-home advertising: Any exposure to advertising occurring outside of one's home.

pay per click (PPC): Pricing model in which advertising fees are determined based on the number of users who click on an online ad or email.

photoboards: Photographs made from a televised commercial and accompanied by a script; intended as record keeping by an agency or client.

pitch: Act of presenting an advertising concept to a prospective or current client.

pop-up ad: Disruptive online ad appearing on top of content already on the computer screen.

portfolio: Collection of samples done by a creative professional or agency used to acquire work or promote that agency. Also called a *book*.

preferred position: Advertising position that is thought to attract the most attention and is sold at a higher rate, e.g., the back cover of a magazine.

print advertising: Advertising printed in a magazine, newspaper, catalog, etc., generally including a mix of photography, illustration, and *copy*.

pro bono: Work done for free, typically by an ad agency on behalf of a nonprofit organization.

production: Actual creation of an ad for print, broadcast, or online use.

product placement: Clear mention or display of a product in a non-advertising portion of a show, movie, etc., e.g., a character in a movie drinking from a Pepsi can.

promotion: Advertising that uses extra values such as temporary discounts, coupons, and contests.

proof: Penultimate version of a print ad piece for the purpose of checking copy and color correctness and quality of the material.

psychographics: Characterization of consumers on the basis of psychological profiles determined through standardized tests. See also *demographics*.

public relations (PR): Generating and maintaining a brand, product, or company image through communication with the public and media to influence attitudes and opinions.

public service advertising: Advertising addressing an issue of public interest, generally sponsored by a nonprofit, civic, political, trade, or religious group.

rate: Amount charged by a media company to an advertiser based on space purchased; can be either fixed or variable. Media companies will generally use their highest rate on their published *rate card*.

rate card: A media campaign's published prices for advertising. Used to promote rates and services.

reach: Estimated audience that sees something at least once over a specific period.

readership: Total number of readers of a publication.

recall: Measure of the amount of people who remember seeing or being exposed to a specific ad after the fact. May be aided ("Do you remember seeing a Tylenol ad?") or unaided ("What medicine ads have you seen lately?").

residuals: Amount paid to a performer for each time a broadcast commercial is run.

retouching: Alterations made to improve photographs, artwork, or film.

return on investment (ROI): Measure of the success of an advertising program, typically calculated in financial terms based on generated revenue.

road blocking: Strategy for scheduling advertisements on multiple broadcast stations or websites with the aim of making it impossible for a consumer not to see the ad.

rough cut: Low-quality, inexpensive cut of film or video edited together with a rough soundtrack to represent the finished product to a client for approval before costs are incurred in mastering the final version.

sales representative: Person soliciting goods or services through direct-marketing means.

search engine marketing: Marketing strategy enabling a company to optimize its website through key word coding, copyediting changes, and the use of reciprocal links to enhance popularity in search engine indexing and rank.

shoot: Act of filming or photography for a commercial or print ad.

skyscraper: Long, thin ad generally placed horizontally on a website.

slogan: Short, memorable phrase, such as "Just do it," that helps in recall and identification of an ad, brand, or product. See also *tagline*.

social network: Website whose prime use is to connect people and allow them to share personal information with others.

spot advertising: Advertising presented in select locations on a market-to-market basis rather than a national level.

spread: Ad printed on or across two facing pages in a magazine.

storyboard: Series of roughly drawn panels and captions depicting the concept for a TV commercial; presented to the client for approval before any large costs are incurred.

tagline: Visual display of a *slogan*.

talent: Actors, models, voice-overs, and others featured in an ad.

targeted advertising: Use of market research to place ads in locations highly trafficked by a target market.

target market: Advertiser's intended audience based on their likelihood to use the product or service.

teaser campaign: Campaign intended to generate public interest and curiosity before a product is on the market.

testing: Market research conducted to identify the strongest concept out of several options for a campaign; may involve focus groups, surveys, or questionnaires directed at a specific target demographic.

touch points: Television, radio, print, online, posters, billboards, publicity events: any and all of the forms an ad campaign takes to reach the consumer.

trade character: Advertising icons identifiable with specific products, e.g., the Energizer Bunny.

transit advertising: Advertisements appearing at train stations, waiting areas, and bus stops, as well as on public transportation vehicles.

uniques: Number of different individuals who have visited a particular website or webpage.

up-front buys: Purchasing of both broadcast and print space early in a buying season, typically to lock in a more favorable rate.

vertical marketing: Creating multiple versions of an advertising message for specific niche audiences based on profession, interest, market category, etc.

viral marketing: Low-budget marketing technique in which a product is made popular by word-of-mouth exposure and sharing over the Internet. A group of consumers see an ad or information on a product and share it with their friends, who share it with their friends, and so on.

wear out: Point where an advertising campaign loses its effectiveness due to repeated public exposure.

Web 2.0: Buzzword describing the current level of online interactivity allowing information to be shared and commented on more quickly, more easily, and more widely than before. Harbingers of this new generation include activities such as blogging, search engine optimizing, and tagging and services such as YouTube, Flickr, and Wikipedia.

white space: Unfilled space in a print advertisement, including between blocks of type, illustrations, headlines, etc.

CAREER-PLANNING WORKBOOK

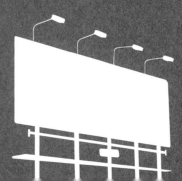

MY CONTACTS

Keep notes about all the people you add to your network—if you're meeting as many people as you should, you won't be able to remember all their details! When you reconnect with someone a few days, weeks, or months after your initial meeting, a brief reminder of where and how you met will make it more likely that you'll get a response. Keep track of the email correspondence you have with these contacts: Start a folder in your email program titled *Job Search*, and stash all your messages there in case you need to refer to them later.

Name: Ed Gonzalez; gonzaleze@email.com

Company: JWT

Title/Department: Copywriter

Where We Met: Adweek event--9/22. We talked about what it was like in the industry; living in New York vs. Texas, where we're both from

Follow-ups: Emailed him on 9/24; sent a copy of my résumé for critique. Received response on 9/28; he said to email again when I'm looking for fulltime work.

Notes: Ed is from outside of College Station; went to school in the northeast, but big Aggies fan

Name: _____

Company: _____

Title/Department: _____

Where We Met: _____

_____

Follow-ups: _____

_____

Notes: _____

_____

~~~~~~

Name: _____

Company: _____

Title/Department: _____

Where We Met: _____

_____

Follow-ups: _____

_____

Notes: _____

_____

Name: _____

Company: _____

Title/Department: _____

Where We Met: _____

_____

Follow-ups: _____

_____

Notes: _____

_____

~~~~~~

Name: _____

Company: _____

Title/Department: _____

Where We Met: _____

_____

Follow-ups: _____

_____

Notes: _____

_____

Name:

Company:

Title/Department:

Where We Met:

Follow-ups:

Notes:

~~~~~~

Name:

Company:

Title/Department:

Where We Met:

Follow-ups:

Notes:

Name: _____

Company: _____

Title/Department: _____

Where We Met: _____

_____

Follow-ups: _____

_____

Notes: _____

_____

~~~~~~

Name: _____

Company: _____

Title/Department: _____

Where We Met: _____

_____

Follow-ups: _____

_____

Notes: _____

_____

Name: _____

Company: _____

Title/Department: _____

Where We Met: _____

_____

Follow-ups: _____

_____

Notes: _____

_____

~~~~~~

Name: _____

Company: _____

Title/Department: _____

Where We Met: _____

_____

Follow-ups: _____

_____

Notes: _____

_____

COMPANY RESEARCH

BONUS TIP: Start a folder on your computer where you store electronic copies of any articles or press releases about the company.

Got an interview coming up? Knock their socks off by showing just how much you know about the company and its projects. After you impress them with your expertise, how could they help but hire you? You can also use these pages to collect research on any companies you'd *like* to be interviewing at someday.

Company: Golden Retriever

Contact: Sylvia Fletcher, founder; fletchers@gretriever.com

History: Founded by Fletcher 3 years ago after she left O&M as Creative Director. Prides itself on cutting edge online work using nontraditional resources like social network sites and YouTube.

Major Competitors: Similar agencies in the boutique mode include Wicked Media and Smith and Court

Significant Projects: "Say it all" campaign for Walking Global Communications was nominated for a Clio last year

Recent News: Just given full control of Direct Territory's advertising; plans to expand their NY offices. May be hiring soon!!!

Other Notes: Fletcher has mentioned in interviews how large agencies can be good intro to the business; play up internship at W+K

Company: _____

Contact: _____

History: _____

_____

Major Competitors: _____

Significant Projects: _____

Recent News: _____

_____

Other Notes: _____

_____

~~~~~~

Company: _____

Contact: _____

History: _____

_____

Major Competitors: _____

Significant Projects: _____

Recent News: _____

_____

Other Notes: _____

_____

Company: _____

Contact: _____

History: _____

_____

Major Competitors: _____

Significant Projects: _____

Recent News: _____

_____

Other Notes: _____

_____

~~~~~~

Company: _____

Contact: _____

History: _____

_____

Major Competitors: _____

Significant Projects: _____

Recent News: _____

_____

Other Notes: _____

_____

RÉSUMÉ WARM-UP

List the classes, jobs, and experiences you've had that demonstrate your proficiency in the following areas. (For more specific guidelines, see Chapter 3. Remember, your experiences don't all have to be industry related! During your three years as a customer service rep at the Apple store, you learned valuable people and communication skills that can transfer to any job.

On the following pages, write down whatever you can think of, even if you're not entirely sure it's applicable. You can always choose to focus on certain jobs and experiences when you actually write your résumé.

Communication Skills

Computer/Technical Skills

_____

_____

_____

_____

_____

_____

_____

_____

_____

_____

_____

_____

Organizational/Office Skills

_____

_____

_____

_____

_____

_____

_____

_____

_____

_____

_____

_____

_____

_____

People Skills

Creative Skills

_____

_____

_____

_____

_____

_____

_____

_____

_____

_____

_____

_____

_____

_____

Business Skills

Strategic/Analytical Skills

RÉSUMÉ ACTION WORDS

Your résumé is a marketing tool, so strive to make it a compelling advertisement for yourself. After you've written down all your relevant experience, use the list of key words below to make your work sound as active and impressive as possible (without lying, of course!).

Also make sure to break down your job into specific duties. Rather than just listing "Camp Counselor" on your résumé and calling it a day, take a few extra minutes to articulate everything you were responsible for: *Supervised thirty 10–12-year-olds; coordinated daily swim sessions and sports events; developed three-month leadership program for older students; wrote weekly newsletter for parents.*

accelerated	designed	led	reorganized
activated	devised	maintained	reported
adapted	directed	managed	represented
administered	documented	mastered	researched
analyzed	drafted	maximized	responsible
applied	edited	modeled	reviewed
approved	eliminated	modified	revised
arranged	established	motivated	scheduled
assembled	evaluated	negotiated	set up
assisted	examined	organized	shaped
built	executed	operated	simplified
compiled	expanded	overhauled	solicited
completed	facilitated	oversaw	solved
composed	formulated	participated	streamlined
conceived	founded	performed	structured
conceptualized	generated	planned	supervised
conducted	guided	prepared	supported
consolidated	handled	presented	surveyed
constructed	illustrated	produced	synthesized
consulted	implemented	programmed	taught
contributed	improved	promoted	tested
controlled	increased	proposed	trained
coordinated	initiated	proved	translated
created	interacted	publicized	utilized
critiqued	interpreted	published	volunteered
delegated	introduced	recommended	worked
developed	launched	reduced	wrote

INTERVIEW WARM-UP

During your interviews, it's pretty much guaranteed that the following questions will pop up—a lot. So prepare your answers now, before you're in the hot seat.

Tell me about yourself.

_____

_____

_____

_____

_____

Why do you want to go into the advertising industry?

_____

_____

_____

_____

Make sure you tailor your answers to the specific company you're interviewing for!

What do you know about our company?

_____

_____

_____

_____

Why do you want to work at this company?

_____

_____

_____

_____

_____

What are some of your favorite ads? Why?

_____

_____

_____

_____

_____

What are your strengths?

_____

_____

_____

_____

_____

What are your weaknesses?

_____

_____

_____

_____

When and how do you do your best work?

_____

_____

_____

Tell me about a time when you had to overcome a difficult situation.

_____

_____

_____

What inspires you?

_____

_____

_____

_____

Tell me about your internships.

_____

_____

_____

_____

Where do you see yourself in five years?

_____

_____

_____

_____

_____

Do you have any questions for me?

_____

_____

_____

_____

_____

_____

Your 5 Talking Points

Interviews often go by in a big blur, and 30 minutes later you're standing in the lobby thinking, *What just happened?* Learn from the politicians: Before you walk into an interview, think of the five things you most want to emphasize. Maybe it's the fact that you handled a full courseload while juggling two part-time jobs. Maybe it's the fact that you wrote your senior essay on marketing and new media. Maybe it's the great transferable skills you gained volunteering at the animal shelter. Whatever they are, note them here. But don't go crazy and list everything impressive about yourself! Force yourself to focus on the most important things.

1. _____

2. _____

3. _____

4. _____

5. _____

Your 30-Second Biography

Sometimes, you don't get much time to make a big impression. Can you paint a vivid, compelling portrait of yourself in less than a minute? Write your 30-second biography in the space below. Memorize it. Use it.

_____

_____

_____

_____

_____

INTERNSHIP TRACKING SHEET

Date	Company	Department	Contact Name	Contact Info	Reference Name	Activity	Next Step

JOB SEARCH TRACKING SHEET

Date	Company	Department	Contact Name	Contact Info	Reference Name	Activity	Next Step

ABOUT THE AUTHOR

Randi Zuckerberg is marketing director of Facebook, where she manages some of the company's larger deals and client relationships; develops new advertising materials, promotions, and programs; documents the company's growth through film; and strives to keep up with the college kids and recent grads. A native New Yorker, Randi is a graduate of Harvard University, where she received her BA in Psychology. Before joining Facebook, she worked in account management at Ogilvy & Mather and Forbes, Inc. When she's not running really long distances, Randi loves singing and musical theater.

ACKNOWLEDGMENTS

Special thanks to my editor, Andrew Sylvester, for his incredible patience, intelligence, and sense of humor that made the writing process so much fun. Thanks to Josh Cracraft for seeking me out and getting everything off to such a great start and to Emma Chastain for her valuable assistance with the manuscript. Thanks as well to Nina Rastogi, creator and brains behind this great series. Thanks to Jill Rothman, whose expert review helped to fine-tune this book, and Ty Montague, whose unique insight into the industry proved very valuable. Thanks to my sister, Donna Zuckerberg (the best writer I know), my mom, Karen Zuckerberg, and the rest of my wonderful family (Mark, Arielle, and Edward). Much appreciation to Shari Miller, Margot Kaminski, Jessica Melore, Stephanie Wang, Radhika Dewan, Paul Fombelle, Bruce Rogers, Hazel Grace Dircksen, and everyone I contacted through Facebook for their time and guidance and to the many advertising industry professionals who contributed quotes, stories, and advice. I'd like to dedicate this book to Brent Tworetzky, my muse and inspiration, who put up with my weekends of writing and ignoring him, always with a smile and loving support.